Bringing the High/Scope Approach to your Early Years Practice

This easy-to-read series provides an introduction to some of the most important early years philosophies and shows how they can be incorporated into your setting. Each book provides:

- An outline of the background to the approach

- Clear explanations of the relevance to contemporary thinking

- Suggestions to help you to plan a successful learning environment

- Examples of what the individual approach can look like in practice.

These convenient guides are essential to early years practitioners, students and parents who wish to fully understand what each approach means to their setting and children.

Have you ever wondered what High/Scope is, where it came from and how it can be used with young children in your setting?

Bringing the High/Scope Approach to your Early Years Practice provides an introduction to the High/Scope philosophy and its use in early years. This new edition has been fully updated to show how the High/Scope approach links with the Early Years Foundation Stage and contains new material on working with the under twos.

Features include:

- Details about the High/Scope wheel of learning
- An explanation of active learning, including materials, manipulation, choice, language and support
- Plan-do-review activities
- Planning and assessment methods.

This convenient guide will help early years practitioners, students and parents to really understand what the High/Scope approach can offer their setting and children.

Nicky Holt has been using the High/Scope approach for the past 14 years, both as a practitioner and as a trainer.

Bringing the High/ Scope Approach to your Early Years Practice

---

SECOND EDITION

Nicky Holt
Series edited by Sandy Green

Routledge
Taylor & Francis Group

LONDON AND NEW YORK

This second edition published 2010
by Routledge
2 Park Square, Milton Park, Abingdon, Oxon, OX14 4RN

Simultaneously published in the USA and Canada
by Routledge
270 Madison Avenue, New York, NY 10016

Routledge is an imprint of the Taylor & Francis Group, an informa business

© 2010 Nicky Holt

Typeset in Optima by
Pindar NZ, Auckland, New Zealand
Printed and bound in Great Britain by
TJ International Ltd, Padstow, Cornwall

British Library Cataloguing in Publication Data
A catalogue record for this book is available from the British Library

Library of Congress Cataloging in Publication Data
Holt, Nicky.
Bringing the high/scope approach to your early years practice / Nicky Holt.
— 2nd ed.
    p. cm.
Includes bibliographical references.
1. Early childhood education—Great Britain. 2. Active learning—Great
Britain. I. Title.
    LB1139.3.G7H65 2010
    372.210941—dc22   2009046328

ISBN10: 0-415-56499-9 (hbk)
ISBN10: 0-415-56500-6 (pbk)
ISBN10: 0-203-85179-X (ebk)

ISBN13: 978-0-415-56499-1 (hbk)
ISBN13: 978-0-415-56500-4 (pbk)
ISBN13: 978-0-203-85179-1 (ebk)

Contents

Acknowledgements   vi

1 Introduction and background   1

2 The physical environment   13

3 Resources   39

4 High/Scope with infants and toddlers   70

5 How High/Scope links to the Early Years Foundation Stage   90

Appendix   116

References, further reading and training opportunities   121

Acknowledgements

To my parents who supported and encouraged me to follow my desire to train and work with young children many years ago, especially Mum who continued to work to pay for me to travel to college and buy all the books I needed to complete my training.

To Stevie, who introduced me formally to High/Scope and set me on my own active learning journey.

To all the children I have worked with over the past 29 years who have inspired, challenged and amazed me all at the same time and continue to do so.

To Sandy who respected and believed in my knowledge and ability to write books that others would want to read – thank you.

To my work colleagues who constantly gave support in their own way – here we are finally published!

Finally (but by no means least) to my wonderful daughters Finola and Sophie for being who you are; for being my rocks and inspiration through some tough times and again allowing me to use your childhood artwork throughout this book.

To my wonderful daughters Finola and Sophie – you have taught me so much over the years and I love you both.

1 | Introduction and background

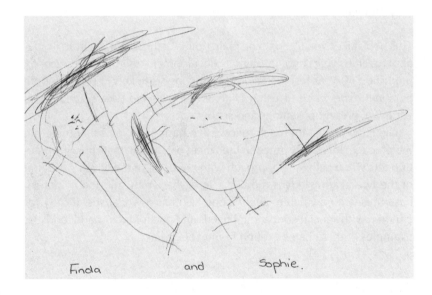

Finda   and   Sophie.

Educating young children means providing them with ongoing opportunities for active learning. Young children in action develop initiative, curiosity, resourcefulness and self confidence – dispositions that serve them well throughout their lives.

(Hohmann and Weikart 2002: 2)

Have you ever seen the words 'High/Scope' and wondered what it meant or was all about? Well I hope this book will answer your questions and more.

So what does High/Scope mean?

High = the individual level of achievement we wish for all children in our care to be able to achieve.

Scope = the range (scope) of experiences we can offer to children to support them to achieve their personal 'high'.

This book takes you through the main points of the approach from its creation over 40 years ago, through its development and up to the recently published 40-year research study. The theory is linked to practice from personal experience of using High/Scope over the past 13 years in a variety of preschool settings and schools.

The High/Scope approach follows five basic principles that underpin the practice; this is illustrated in the wheel of learning that supports practitioners when using the approach with children. In the UK the addition of the tyre acknowledges the key role of the family and the evidence-based research available. High/Scope also has a wheel specifically for children with special educational needs and one for infants and toddlers. Examples of these can be found in the appendix.

An overview of each of the segments of the High/Scope wheel

Active learning

This is the way children learn – actively! They find out for themselves what something is like by using their senses and this is seen from birth through childhood and on into adult life. Children use their initiative to explore and seek out answers to their questions. They are supported to

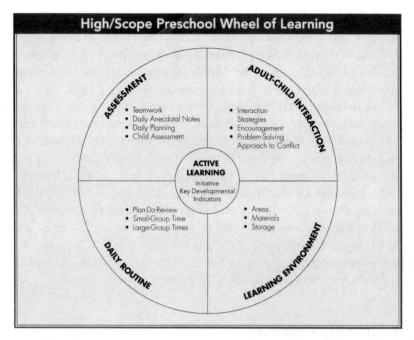

High/Scope Preschool Wheel of Learning

Reproduced with kind permission from High/Scope UK © 2007.
High/Scope UK.

solve their own problems and use their growing knowledge to understand and learn from the world around them.

This was graphically illustrated in the following example: When working with a group of young children aged 2–3 years in early spring, talking about rabbits and enjoying the story of Peter Rabbit together. During a small-group time the children were asked to draw some pictures of a rabbit to add to the setting's spring display. The resulting drawings were fine although mainly circular scribbles with no clear definition, typical of children of this age group. The next day two pet rabbits, Toffee and Treacle, were brought into the nursery. The rabbits were introduced to the children at circle time and a discussion began about their food, what they liked doing, where they lived etc. The children were allowed to handle the rabbits as much as they liked. (Fortunately the rabbits were two extremely laid-back pets that were very used to being handled!)

Later in the day at small-group time the children began to draw pictures of Toffee and Treacle, the resulting pictures were really amazing. These 2–3-year-olds were drawing oval bodies with legs, pointy ears, whiskers and fluffy tails! This was an awakening moment for staff to the power of active learning and the High/Scope approach for young children.

'Key developmental indicators', in the centre of the wheel, illustrate what children of all ages and abilities can do and how they learn from and make sense of the world around them. These indicators are what High/Scope practitioners use to record their observations of children at work and are grouped into five categories: Approaches to learning, Language, Literacy and communication, Social and emotional development, Physical development, Health and well-being and Arts and science. Arts and science is subdivided into mathematics, science and technology, social studies and the arts.

The indicators are seen as the building blocks of thinking and reasoning at each stage of development.

Adult/child interaction

The adults working with children provide the safe environment essential for active learning to take place. In a High/Scope setting, using a process of shared control, adults and children work together in mutual respect, focusing on the children's strengths with a balance of adult-directed and child-initiated activities. Adults are seen as supporters of children's learning and fully engage with children in 'their' world. Practitioners have spent many times in the 'home' area, for example being the 'baby' or going to the 'hairdressers' and having their hair washed, dried, brushed and then done with ribbons and clips. For practitioners with very short hair that's no mean feat for the creative children we work with!

Practitioners in the High/Scope setting use encouragement rather than praise with the young children they work with. They believe comments specific to the child's actions, for example 'you used the red bricks to build your wall' rather than 'well done you've made a good job of that' allows a child to feel good about their achievements. Studies show that praise ... invites comparison and competition and increases the child's dependence on adults. Encouragement however, puts children in control and makes them evaluators of their own work.

(Tomkins 1991, in Hohmann and Weikart 2002: 242)

In a High/Scope setting conflict is seen as another learning opportunity. Adults and children use a problem-solving approach to support their understanding of the issues; it also helps adults to see children as problem solvers not problems to be solved. High/Scope practitioners follow the 'six steps to conflict resolution' in their work with children which are laid out below.

1. Approach the situation calmly

   Watch what is going on and try to be positive. Keep the voice at normal conversational level and use facial expression to show displeasure. Sit or kneel at the children's level and reach out to the upset child allowing them to come to you.

2. Recognise the children's feelings

   'You look sad, Joe, and you sound angry, Sam.'

3. Gather information and restate the problem

   Listen to both children and ask questions to help everyone understand the issue. 'So you had the ball, Joe, and Sam, you would like to play with it too?'

4. Ask for ideas/solutions

   'What can we do about this?' Support and encourage the children to talk to each other. 'We could find another ball.'

5. Retell any suggested solutions

   Accept the children's suggested solution. 'So you're going to find another ball.'

6. Support children to act on their decision

   Give encouragement to the children as they manage their problem and stay close to clarify the decisions made if necessary.

The learning environment

As in all early years settings how the play environment is set out is of importance. In High/Scope settings the room/s will be set out in areas to support children's choices and interest. They provide easy access to a range of materials both man-made and natural to support the children's independent learning; if children know where to find something they can fetch it for themselves and become confident in their abilities. Outside areas are seen as an extension to the inside learning environment and should be available to the children throughout their working time.

The benefits of this were demonstrated to a parent being shown around the nursery who was questioning why she should bring her son to the High/Scope nursery rather than the local preschool. During their conversation they were interrupted by a 3-year-old girl: 'Look Nicky, I've dropped sand,' she said looking at a pile of sand on the floor. Nicky asked, 'Oh, what shall we do about that?' to which the girl went over to the nearby sink, collected the dust pan and brush which was hanging there and began to sweep up the sand. After a short while she looked up with a smile and said, 'Look I've done it.' 'You've swept the sand,' Nicky replied. The learning environment empowered this child to manage her own problem with very little adult support.

The daily routine

The High/Scope routine is consistent. This provides security for children who soon learn to predict what comes next and can plan their time accordingly. Children have time to work alone during 'plan-do-review', and in small and large groups, thus encouraging them to build a community in which they have a rightful place. A sample daily routine for a two-and-a-half-hour group might look a little like this:

> **Greeting time** – provides a smooth transition between home and school/nursery

Large-group time – children and adults gather to share information about the day/session, tell stories, play group games, sing songs, dance and play instruments

Small-group time – adult-initiated, activity is presented and the children choose how they use the materials

Planning time – children indicate what they wish to do in work time, what they may use and who they may play with

Work (do) time – children carry out their plans and adults interact with the children by extending their play, encouraging their thinking, developing their language and supporting problem solving

Tidy-up time – children and adults work together to tidy away the materials

Review time – children talk about what they have been doing and can show their work to others

Snack time – children are offered a drink and healthy snack while lots of conversations are going on

Large-group time – songs and endings

Parents collect

Assessment

Through regular observation, interaction with and recording of what children can do early years practitioners build a store of children's interests and skills that they use to inform their planning for small- and large-group times. Practitioners are encouraged to share observations with each other, record using the key developmental indicators and share this with the parents/carers. Using the High/Scope Child Observation Records

(COR) gives a structured platform that shows individual progression through the early learning goals and developmental milestones.

Parents and carers are usually very interested in the assessments made by practitioners; it gives them another avenue into their children's lives. They love to take home their child's record and read what they are able to do; it enhances their relationship with their child. Parents are often amazed at how much their children are able to do and are capable of at a very young age.

Underpinning the whole approach is a commitment to empower children although many feel it empowers all who embrace its philosophy: staff, parents and students alike.

So where did it all start and why?

High/Scope was developed by Dr David Weikart in America in the early 1960s. David Weikart was an ex-marine who studied at the University of Michigan in the late 1950s. He became a school psychologist and director of special services for the public school system in Ypsilanti. He was a young man keen to take on the challenges of education at that time.

There were significant issues for children from lower-class society and especially African-American children at this time. In Ypsilanti all African-American families were housed in a single neighbourhood therefore attending the same elementary school, common practice in America in the 1950s. In this segregated elementary school children were shown to be low achievers and standard testing showed they had low IQ scores, whereas the same-age children in predominantly white areas achieved considerably higher attainment scores. When David Weikart questioned this he was met with 'everything possible was already being done .... what could you expect? Their ability was what they were born with' (Weikart 2004: 48).

Undeterred he continued to work with the school system and discovered children who lived in the deprived neighbourhoods in Ypsilanti were achieving low scores as a result of lack of opportunity rather than intelligence levels and early (preschool) intervention was seen as the best way to improve this.

The Perry Preschool Project

In 1962 the Perry Preschool Project began; children from the Perry Elementary School area were randomly selected to attend either the High/Scope project or stay in the community/home with their families. It was vital for the project to have a control group for comparison, to measure if being in a preschool setting made a difference to these children. The project had three basic criteria:

- A coherent theory about teaching and learning must guide the development of a curriculum for children.

- Curriculum theory and practice must support each child's capacity to develop individual talents and abilities through ongoing opportunities for active learning.

- The teachers, researchers and administrators must work as partners in all aspects of the curriculum development, to ensure that theory and practice receive equal consideration.

(Bell 2004: 5).

The project staff looked at the writings of Jean Piaget and were drawn to his theories on child development and how they supported the team's orientation towards active learning. After much debate the basic framework of the High/Scope curriculum was born, with active learning at its core and the belief that children learn through key experiences gained from the world around them and from their own discoveries. The project also felt that parents played a key role in their children's early years; therefore home visits were set up where teachers offered ideas about child development and learning. Engaging with the parents this way became a two-way process because it gave the parents an opportunity to pass on things about the individual child's interests and family.

Initial results from the Perry Preschool project showed that the children made great strides in improving their IQ score when entering into mainstream schooling: 'Poor children could move on from the preschool to elementary school better able to engage in traditional education' (Weikart 2004: 55).

It was decided to track the children who attended the project between 1962 and 1967 through their education and beyond to ascertain the benefits of High/Scope throughout life. Information was collected annually on 123 students from aged 3 to 11 years and then at 14, 15, 19, 27 and 40 years. Below is a summary of the findings at age 27.

Dr Weikart and his team continued to develop the High/Scope approach and in 1970 established the High/Scope Educational Research Foundation. The foundation continued to develop High/Scope through the years to the approach we use today and continues to produce materials for use in High/Scope settings. It also supports the continued research into High/Scope, most recently carrying out and producing the Lifetime Effects 40-year study. This also produced results showing the substantial benefits to children who have experienced the High/Scope approach into their adult life.

The benefits of the High/Scope approach as outlined in the current research is also upheld by the recent Effective Provision of Preschool Education (EPPE) study from the UK. This highlights the benefits to children, especially disadvantaged children, of good-quality preschool experiences which can be found in the High/Scope approach. The EPPE project found these elements important:

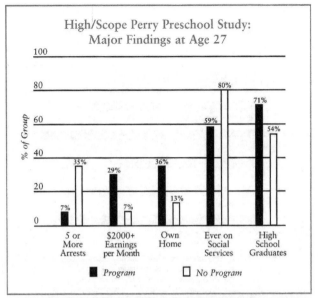

High/Scope Perry Preschool Study: Major Findings at Age 27

From *Educating Young Children (p. 8)* by Mary Hohmann and David P. Weikart, Ypsilanti, MI:High/Scope Press.
© 2002 High/Scope Educational Research Foundation
Used with permission

● the quality of adult-child interaction – a feature of High/Scope and its philosophy of shared control between adult and child

● initiation of activities – High/Scope has both child-initiated time (plan-do-review) and adult-initiated (small-group time) where support can be given to children

● knowledge about how children learn – training in the approach and especially the key experiences support practitioners to learn from the children themselves

● High levels of parental engagement in children's learning – in a High/Scope setting the relationship with the parents is fostered through initial two-way information sharing and then continues with the sharing of the child observation records and offering of parent workshops.

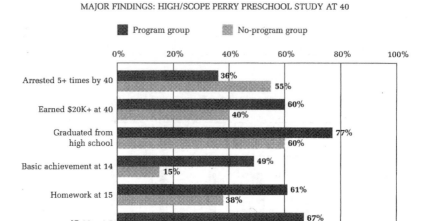

MAJOR FINDINGS: HIGH/SCOPE PERRY PRESCHOOL STUDY AT 40

From Lifetime Effects, The High/Scope Perry Preschool Study Through Age 40 (p. xv)
by Lawrence J. Schweinhart et al.,
MI:High/Scope Press. © 2005 High/Scope
Educational Research Foundation.
Used with permission

● A discipline/behaviour policy which supports children in rationalising and talking through their conflicts – in High/Scope the use of encouragement and a problem-solving approach to conflict between children is promoted.

Evidence from both the High/Scope Lifetime Effects 40-year study and the UK EPPE project shows what a substantial and beneficial approach for all children High/Scope is. For practitioners working with young children having this supportive background guides them in their ongoing work, not only today but for the future.

2 | The physical environment

A High/Scope setting will initially look very similar to any good-quality early years setting and in this chapter we will go through the unique differences in how it is set up and used by both adults and children.

As outlined previously the High/Scope approach follows five basic principles that underpin the whole approach, illustrated in the wheel of learning. At its core is active learning; the belief that active learning is essential for the development of all children and adults is deep-seated

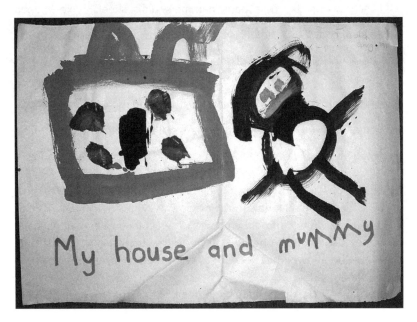

within the approach. It is learning that happens when the child interacts with objects, people and events around them and builds new understanding from them. No one can have or experience things for another; only individuals can have and learn from experiences for themselves.

Active learning

> Active learning is defined as learning in which the child, by acting on objects and interacting with people, ideas and events, constructs new understanding.
>
> (Hohmann and Weikart 2002: 17)

In a High/Scope setting we support children on their voyage of active learning by providing five basic ingredients:

Materials – A plentiful variety of interesting materials, bought or found, for children to play with. This might include:

- Everyday objects – pots, pans, hammers, nails, sheets, boxes, paper

- Natural materials – stones, shells, leaves, twigs, pebbles etc.

- Tools – brushes, mops, scissors, staplers, paper clips, hoses, watering cans

- Messy items – water, soap, playdough, clay, paint

- Large, heavy items – big blocks, planks of wood, boxes, crates, bikes

- Smaller items – Lego, buttons, toy cars, pasta, beads, small figures.

Manipulation – offering opportunities to and allowing children to explore and work with the materials in their own way.

Choice – giving children the choice to select their own materials and how they use them. If children are to follow their desire for learning they must be allowed the freedom to choose activities and materials to support that learning.

Language – from the child. Children talk about what they are doing or have done, reflect on their learning, integrate new knowledge and build relationships with others.

Support – from the adults. Adults support and extend children's efforts by talking with them about what they are doing, asking what High/Scope calls real questions, ones they don't already know the answer to. Joining in with their play and supporting them to solve problems.

By using the five ingredients above as often as possible with children in their play experiences we support their voyage of discovery and learning and have fun together along the way too.

For adults to understand active learning and its importance in how children learn, it is best to experience it for themselves. Here is an example of how it is often presented to adults in training sessions.

In a taster session for adults on active learning a High/Scope trainer/ facilitator would present the participants with some apples (some red, some green), this is something the majority of people are familiar with. Everyone would be able to choose an apple and for about five minutes explore it using all their five senses – touch, hearing, sight, smell and taste. There would also be plates, knives and some kitchen towel already on hand for participants to use as and if they wished. Each person would have a piece of paper and a pen and would be asked to record everything they discover about an apple. Whilst they are exploring the fruit the facilitator would acknowledge what individuals are saying and comment or offer new words; they would also be there to support them to work through any problems they may encounter along the way. After exploring the apples, participants and facilitator would record onto a flip chart every thing or word that had been discovered, for example, juicy, crunchy, spotty, have pips, round, smooth, wet inside, tasty, smell clean, can roll. Participants would then be offered some plastic apples and would go through the list and cross off all the things not found out by just exploring the plastic fruit. The facilitator would then use a picture of an apple and the word APPLE and go through the whole process twice more. At this point all the words from the exploration exercise have usually been crossed out! This is often when the realisation of what people have experienced hits them.

It is important to use something familiar as adults often think they know everything about an object, therefore the power of active learning, what they found out through exploration, is much more evident and clear to them.

By allowing the adults to explore the fruit in any way they wanted they discovered so much more than from the plastic fruit, picture or word. All of us, but especially children, learn by having real experiences. Children won't learn about an apple or a rabbit, for example, by looking at a picture but the picture will be meaningful if the children have had first-hand experience of the fruit or rabbit. By experiencing an apple and building up knowledge of the fruit a child can use this knowledge and understanding to inform them about other new objects and experiences they have.

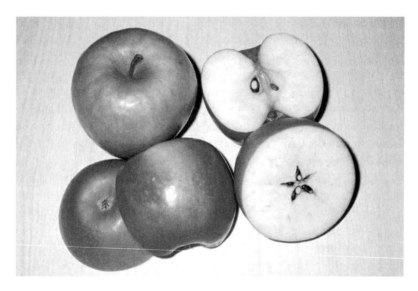

We have all witnessed the learning that a young baby goes through when it discovers its own feet or hands: the frowns on its face as the foot or hand comes into focus; the way it immediately plays with the fingers or toes, feeling the skin and then guiding the foot or hand into its mouth for further exploration. The baby has to do this for itself; we cannot teach the sensations and learning that is going on for the individual. The baby is experiencing active learning for itself; it instinctively does it. What it learns from its own fingers it can use to understand its parents' hands, its

toys and its food. This way of learning is natural and instinctive and con-tinues throughout our lives and is the core of the High/Scope approach.
The ingredients of active learning flow throughout the exercise:

- **Materials** – enough apples, plates, knives, paper and pens were pro-vided for everyone to have their own.

- **Manipulation** – participants were free to explore the fruit as they wished.

- **Choice** – participants were free to choose which apple they wanted (red or green) or if they wanted one at all. They had choice in what they did with it, what they recorded on the paper and how they described their finding out.

- **Language** – adults freely chatted whilst exploring the fruit and shared words and checked things out with each other and the trainer during the exploration time.

- **Support** – the facilitator was there to support by supplying the apples and equipment and then during their exploration could support problem solving.

From experience of High/Scope this exercise has been presented many times to parents, students and colleagues from various disciplines using a variety of objects including sherbet lemons, daffodils and even a tepee. On every occasion there is a light bulb moment – when understanding of how we learn is realised and suddenly seems so obvious. If some partici-pants still seem to be a little unsure of the power of active learning other examples can be presented verbally to make it more real for individuals, for example asking them to think back to when they learnt to drive and try to remember how many times they stalled the car before they got the fine balance of clutch control and acceleration. No matter how many times the instructor explains or even tells you what to do, until you are in the driving seat and are using the pedals yourself you cannot truly understand and learn how to drive. To learn to drive you have to have all the ingredients of active learning present:

- **materials** – the car

- **manipulation** – you have to manipulate the controls to make the car go

- **choice** – whether you learn to drive or not

- **language** – lots of chat between you and the instructor

- **support** – the instructor is there to support your learning.

Using an example that feels more real or personal to participants often helps reinforce the understanding of the process for young children.

For children the power of active learning comes from personal initiative. Children act on their innate desire to explore. Think back to the young baby exploring its hands and feet: nobody told the baby to explore them, it just did. As children grow they ask and search for answers to questions: 'Why do I have to put my hat on?' 'What happens if I ...?' They ask questions about people, materials, events in the world around them and ideas that arouse their curiosity, the endless (or so it seems at the time) 'Why?' 'What for?' 'When?' 'How?' They solve problems that stand in the way of their goals and they generate strategies to try. The child who cannot reach something in a cupboard may pull a chair towards it and climb up to reach, or the child who cannot open the garden gate may climb over the fence or look for a hole he could crawl through. Are these children being 'naughty' or defying home rules or are they using their initiative to solve the problems they've encountered?

Children who are active learners become engaged in their play because they have chosen to do so. In a High/Scope setting practitioners will always consider the five factors of intrinsic motivation:

- control

- interest

- enjoyment

- feelings of competence

- probability of success.

Children will become engaged in what they are doing if it is something they are *interested* in, it is *enjoyable* to them, they have *control* over the situation, there is a probability of *success* and they feel *competent* in doing it. For example, Stefan aged 3 years had a great interest in dinosaurs and brought many plastic figures into the nursery. He spent all his work time playing with the dinosaurs in a variety of areas; in the block area he built them homes, while in the art area he drew pictures of them and the environments they lived in and in the book area he made up and told stories about them. Stefan was definitely intrinsically motivated by dinosaurs!

The learning environment

> Environments promoting active learning contain materials that encourage children's exploration and creativity, and plenty of space for children to play alone and with others.
>
> (Hohmann and Weikart 2002: 110)

Areas, materials, storage

In a High/Scope setting the learning environment will be set out in areas where children can play alone or together with other children or adults. The areas should be as large and spacious as possible, should be inviting and welcoming to children and the space divided to encourage differing types of play.

For our youngest children (under 2s) it is equally important to have basic areas where they can play and explore. These are more likely to use fewer physical partitions to allow the babies and toddlers space to explore the environment. Materials should be clean and age-appropriate; use of treasure baskets and heuristic play is more evident for this age of child. Toys and equipment can be stored in a variety of containers, as with the older children, as these can often become something to explore and play with too. We can all, I'm sure, remember an example of how a young child can spend a great deal of time exploring a box and ignoring the contents!

Quiet areas are vital for rest, cuddles and comfort with a familiar adult. These can be filled with easily washable cushions, blankets and if space allows a sofa or large armchair.

The areas are divided by use of a variety of items such as low shelves, furniture and even fencing which can double up as places to store and display the materials that the children have access to. The dividers should be low so that children can see out, they can watch their friends or view where they might like to play next and staff can also scan the room and see the children. The areas are labelled and named with names that not only describe what can be found there but are child-friendly, for example sand and water area, creative/art area, block or construction area, home corner, book/writing area, toy/small-world area, music and movement area. Giving areas a name that means something to children and describes what is available enables the children to feel in control of their own play and develop independence. Staff and children can create clear area signs that can be hung or displayed on the wall at the entrance to the area. These signs usually include the area's name – for example 'block area' or 'block area play' – in words, and pictures, drawings and/or photographs. When using photographs in any setting it is really valuable if the attending children can feature in them; this gives them a sense of ownership of the setting and what goes on there. After all, don't we all enjoy looking at pictures of ourselves? The photographs also demonstrate to parents and carers not only what goes on in the setting but also what their child has been doing.

As children become sure of what is available in the areas they can think ahead and plan their play even before getting to the setting. I have experienced many young children who come to nursery having planned what they wish to do or the area they wish to play in at nursery over the breakfast table with their parents. This is really good for the parents who then have another link into their child's world.

Some areas can be combined if space is limited; for example, sand and water are often in the art area as this makes flooring choices simpler and access to materials and services easier for children. Some areas are sited next to each other as this enables children to use materials from each area in a free-flow way; for example, home area and blocks are often sited together. This allows for play in the home corner, 'we're all a family and have packed our bags and are going on holiday', to flow into the block area, 'we now need to build the car/aeroplane to take us on holiday.' This supports and encourages children to use their imagination and can extend their play. In a High/Scope setting children are free to combine materials to follow their interests, and staff support this by having available other materials as appropriate, to extend the children's learning experience. For example you may often put small-play people from the small-world area into or near the sand so children who have visited the beach may revisit the experience for themselves or share it with friends.

A variety of areas are also available or created in the outside space. Areas for bikes and trucks, space for climbing and jumping, quiet areas for reflection, stories or just chatting with your friends, areas for digging in sand and earth, for growing things. A High/Scope garden or outside space would also include different textures in the ground cover – concrete, paving, wooden slats, grass – and use planting to offer children different experiences of smells, sounds and textures.

Materials within the indoor and outdoor areas are plentiful and varied and offer children a wide range of play experiences. There should be enough to allow several children to play together with the same thing, for example indoors enough pencils to allow several children to draw at the same time and plenty of cars to allow children to play with the garage or on a road map at the same time. I believe it is far more important to have plenty of a smaller range of equipment for several children to play together than a small amount of lots of things. For example five large tubs of construction materials – bricks, Duplo, straws – rather than ten small tubs of a wider range. In this way children develop naturally from solitary play through playing alongside each other to cooperative play.

Outdoors the equipment would again be plentiful and varied and could include bikes/wheeled toys, logs, crates, stones, large pieces of material and wooden planks. Open-ended materials that allow children to follow their interests, as indoors, have a variety of functions and uses. One day some crates and wood could be a car, another day a rocket or house, the only limit being a child's imagination.

Materials on offer to children are a mixture of:

- manufactured toys – Duplo bricks, cars, puzzles, play people, bikes
- recycled materials – newspaper, cardboard, plastic bottles,
- natural materials – stones, fir cones, corks, sponges, wood offcuts, shells
- real items – old toaster, irons, kettles, saws, screwdrivers, dressing-up clothes, whisks, cutlery and crockery.

The lists are endless and only restricted by the setting's ability to source them; materials for children to play with and actively learn from are all around us.

Practitioners and parents can often become concerned about the use of natural and real items in a play setting. The children's safety is paramount at all times; therefore materials selected would be appropriate for the age of the children in the setting. For example, stones would be larger in a baby room than a preschool room, wood offcuts used indoors and especially with babies would have sanded edges and be smooth but outside with the older children could be larger and rougher or natural. With natural materials we must always remember the open-ended nature of them and the play value this has for children. Stones and fir cones can one day be in the home corner being cooked for lunch, on another day in the small-world area representing trees and on another being used to build enclosures for the farm animals. Real items (especially the electrical goods) often cause concern but as long as the cables are cut short and children are supported by the practitioners in the setting to use them appropriately their play value cannot be ignored. Children in the home corner repeatedly take on a role of an adult, often Mum or Dad, and to be able to use the same materials and in the same way as they have seen at home allows them to try out what it's like to be someone else. In the same way that dressing-up enables children to become someone else for a short while, the use of real items also supports this learning.

Materials in the setting should also reflect the community that it serves; having items in the home corner that children will see in their own homes, for example, shows that the children's culture is valued and respected. Children enjoy sharing themselves and this can be done easily through appropriate dressing-up clothes, cooking equipment, pictures and photographs. The materials you provide will also support children's learning about and acceptance of others. The children we work with are growing up in an ever-decreasing world and their horizons are coming closer. If we can in some small way help them on their journey of learning through life we have a duty to do it in the best way possible.

In a High/Scope setting materials are available to the children at all times; this supports children's growing independence and 'I can do it' attitude. It nurtures their self-esteem and confidence to have a go at things at home or in other settings too. This also promotes the find-use-return cycle where children are able to find what they want in an area, use it where and how they want, and then return it to the area where it belongs. If we believe and support children to follow their interests and see them as managers of their own learning we must not hide materials away, so thought must also be given to how we store them.

Low shelves that divide the areas make excellent storage places for equipment relevant to that area and storing similar items together again supports children to find what they need and return it after use, for example blocks in the block area and paint and glue in the art area. This also allows the adults to provide a range of items that could be used for the same thing allowing the individual child to make his own choice; for example, in the art area pencils, felt pens, chalk and wax crayons could all be used for drawing.

The container we use to store things in should be easy to see into, again allowing the child to look around the area and select his or her own materials for play. Containers could be bought or could be old ice-cream tubs, or even plastic milk cartons (with the top cut off); these are especially useful for small things. Flat baskets, old shoe boxes and trays are also useful for children to again see into but are easy to handle. The container can be made from a variety of materials, for example plastic, wicker and cardboard, again reflecting the philosophy of exposing children to a variety of textures.

In areas like the home corner or woodwork area the walls can be used to store things. Items like saucepans, whisks, sieves, spoons, saws, hammers and screwdrivers can all be hung on hooks in the wall. These storage areas should show the picture or outline of the item to be stored or hung there so the children can return items when the play is finished. This again supports the find-use-return cycle and also the development of mathematical concepts. For example, if you have a set of saucepans in graduating sizes (from big to medium down to small) the children can hang the appropriate size pan on the hooks and easily work out for themselves if it matches and then use the correct mathematical language to talk about what they have done.

In areas where boxes can be removed by the children for play it is helpful to have on the shelf a picture and/or word of the item that belongs there. This supports the tidy-up process as children can recognise where things belong, they can compare and match items, and this also has the knock-on effect of helping adults new to the setting or just visiting to see where to put things.

In settings where they share the space with other community groups, for example in village halls, storage of equipment needs to be flexible but at the same time practical. In these settings practitioners need to be creative; large storage boxes or pieces of carpet can be used to divide rooms into the different areas and stand-alone notice boards can be used to display children's work or to pass messages to parents. Shortened hat stands make very good hanging space for dressing-up clothes or painting aprons and small boxes that stack neatly can offer children a range of equipment but are easily packed away at the end of the session.

As we named the areas we also name or label the storage containers and this should be done in a way that has meaning for the children. Labels can use the ways listed below or a combination of these:

- a picture (drawing, photograph or cut from a catalogue) of the item – this helps children to know what is inside the container

- an example of the item, say a car on the car box – this helps not only the very young children but also children with visual impairments or other special needs to play alongside their peers as equals

- the word/name of the item – this support the older children with their emerging letter recognition and reading. Word labels should always have the picture alongside it too.

The labels can be done by hand or on a computer and last much longer if they can be covered with contact paper or laminated. Attaching the labels to the boxes and the shelves with Velcro allows them to be removed easily when you wish to change what is on the shelf or in the box. The removed labels can also be used as a planning prop when carrying out plan-do-review with children or placed along with the shelf labels used as a matching game.

Daily routine

The daily routine provides a common frame work of support for children as they pursue their interests and engage in various problem-solving activities.

(Hohmann and Weikart 2002: 151)

As in any early years setting the daily routine in a High/Scope setting is consistent and flexible at the same time: consistent to offer children security in what comes next and to support their organisation and planning of what they wish to do, but also flexible enough to incorporate unplanned-for events such as being able to go outside to experience a heavy frost or a wonderful spider's web in the garden/outside space.

When working with under 2s it is important to follow their natural routines around feeding and sleeping. A baby room's routine would still have a basic structure but would equally be flexible enough to accommodate individual needs. This can mean that while some babies may be sleeping others could be enjoying a small- or large-group time or even choice time as indicated on the High/Scope wheel of learning for infants and toddlers.

A sample daily routine for an infant/toddler room may look like this:

Arrival – infants and toddlers arrive at times to suit their family's routines

Breakfast – very important for those who arrive early and would incorporate nappy changing as appropriate

Greeting/large-group time – a chance to say hello and share a song or picture book

Choice time – interesting equipment is available for the infants to explore

Small-group time – practitioners and infants gather to enjoy an activity together in a small group

Outside time – infants and toddlers have opportunity to explore beyond their indoor environment

Lunch – a time to sit together socially and share food and chatter and would incorporate nappy changing as appropriate

Nap time – infants, especially those who stay for the whole day, are supported to rest and sleep if they wish.

A routine of activities as above would be planned for the afternoon. Practitioners work flexibly with the youngest children:

> Infant and toddler caregivers strive for an overall daily routine that is predictable – organised and consistent – and still flexible enough to accommodate the needs of individual children.
>
> (Post and Hohmann 2000: 195)

As outlined in Chapter 1 a daily routine for a typical two-and-a-half-hour session would look something like this:

Greeting time – provides a smooth transition between home and school/nursery

Large-group time – children and adults gather to share information about the day/session, tell stories, play group games, sing songs, dance and play instruments

Small-group time – adult-initiated, activity is presented and the children choose how they use the materials

Planning time – children indicate what they wish to do in work time, what they may use and who they may play with

Work (do) time – children carry out their plans and adults interact with the children by extending their play, encouraging their thinking, developing their language and supporting problem solving

Tidy-up time – children and adults work together to tidy away the materials

Review time – children talk about what they have been doing and can show their work to others

Snack time – children are offered a drink and healthy snack while lots of conversations are going on

Large-group time – songs and endings

Parents collect

Let's look at these sections in more detail.

Greeting time

When children arrive at the setting it is so important to be able to greet them and their parent/carer in a calm and relaxed environment. There should always be somewhere big enough to hold the children's outdoor clothes, space where they can leave personal belongings – a drawer or box with their name and their photograph or a picture on it for example. This is another way to support children's self-esteem and independence. It also welcomes them into the setting and gives them a sense of 'I belong here'.

There should be space for parents/carers to pass on information or anecdotes about the child to the setting staff. If space can be provided for parents/carers to meet, chat or just watch their child settle into the routine of the setting this can be very welcomed. This area can also be used for the setting to pass on information about the setting's routines, events, and requests for help with equipment or volunteers on a parent notice board.

A space for children to be able to sign themselves in and out of the setting is also useful and can be done in many ways. For example a board of the children's photos that they find themselves and then bring it into the play space and stick onto another board near the large-group time area; this can then double up as a register of the children in the session that day. Adding the children's names to the pictures helps them to recognise their own name and they often begin to recognise their friends' names too.

Greeting time flows straight into large-group time for the children.

Large-group time

This can often be called 'circle time' in some settings and is a time when all the staff and children meet together to share important information and join in with activities suited to bigger groups. At large-group time messages may be shared, for example staff and children who may be away on holiday or ill, and visitors to the setting that day. During this time a staff member may record the children present in a register to ensure health and safety requirements are met. It is also a good time for a group hello or good morning to everyone. This takes away a more formal register time and supports less confident children to join in. New equipment or tools that will be available to the children to use at work time are often introduced and discussions about issues or problems that may arise.

Large-group time may be used to share stories, sing songs, play instruments and dance. It provides children with enjoyable shared experiences that give them a sense of belonging to a group or community who value each other.

With the youngest children large-group time has the same ethos in that it's a time to say hello, maybe through a song, share musical experiences and simple stories and dance. Babies particularly enjoy simple books made by the practitioner using photographs of themselves and the setting.

Small-group time

Small-group time is the only time in the High/Scope routine when the practitioner would present an activity to children although it's not a teacher-led lesson. The group is made up of the same adult and children each day, often the practitioner and his or her key children. They come together in an intimate setting to explore the materials provided in their own way.

Adults plan small-group times around an interest the children may have or the developmental stage they have reached, for example if the children have a favourite story it could be re-enacted at small-group time or the children could be offered malleable materials to create models for a display about the story. At small-group time the ingredients of active learning are always present:

- **materials** – the children each have their own materials

- **manipulation** – the children can use the materials as they wish

- **choice** – children can make their own choices and decisions about what to do with the materials

- **language** – the children will talk about what they are doing to each other and the adult

- **support** – the adult would move from child to child offering support, encouragement and describing what he/she sees going on.

In a High/Scope setting small-group time builds on what children can do. It introduces them to new materials or materials they may not choose to explore. For example, if you had a child who never did painting because it was messy you may plan a painting small-group time but offer the children a variety of painting utensils such as brushes, sponges and old roll-on deodorant bottles, or even just large buckets of water and a variety of brushes to 'paint' the outside of the building or playground. Small-group time gives staff the opportunity to observe children in the group and listen to their interests; this they can use to write anecdotes to add to the children's development records or to organise the next small-group time.

For the under 2s, small-group time can be a great time to use treasure baskets full of interesting items to explore and investigate. These can be made up of items covering themes such as wood, metal or plastic or focused on a colour or texture. Babies particularly enjoy contrast and black-and-white baskets can prove very popular. In this way the young-est children are introduced to the ingredients of active learning in an instinctive way using their natural need to explore.

Plan-do-review

> In making daily plans, following through on them, and then recalling what they have done, young children learn to articulate their inten-tions and reflect on their actions. They also begin to realise they are competent thinkers, decision makers and problem solvers.
>
> (Hohmann and Weikart 2002: 167)

Plan-do-review is the centrepiece of the High/Scope active learning approach and is the central part of the daily routine. Practitioners give this segment of the daily routine the most time; for example, in a two-and-a-half-hour session plan-do-review will take up at least one of those hours.

Planning time

At planning time children meet in small groups with a familiar adult and plan what they are going to do in the next part of their session. Children can plan in various ways, for example pointing to an activity they wish to do, using photographs of items from the play space, selecting items from areas or as their language skills and confidence develop they often talk about or say what they wish to do. Practitioners may use props to help children to plan such as telephones, puppets and cardboard tubes. These strategies can be particularly useful for children who are reluctant planners or children who find it difficult to communicate with others, who are often more comfortable talking into a phone or to a puppet. Planning with children new to the setting can be carried out in the form of a train that travels around the setting and stops at each area in turn so children wishing to play in that area may jump off; this has the added benefit of supporting the children's learning of the names of the areas. This is also enjoyed by other children who often like to take the role of train driver.

On some occasions the adults may record what the children have planned to do, on others it's accepted verbally. This can often develop into the children writing their own plans with the use of scribbles, words and/or pictures. At planning time children can be encouraged to listen to their peers and await their turn to plan; this can be very hard for the youngest children so it is often best to allow them to move on to the doing stage as soon as they have planned. Planning can also be done on an individual basis with children as they arrive at the setting or during doing time when they change their mind about their initial plan.

Children who attend a High/Scope setting often become so used to the planning process that they enjoy taking the adult's role at planning time. They like to ask the other children what they wish to do, who they want to play with etc. In this shared control environment children develop their confidence and self-esteem in a way that is natural to them.

When children plan they are thinking about what they wish to do and often who they wish to play with; they are turning that thinking into actions and modifying their actions as they go along. Planning is important for children as it encourages them to express their choices, ideas and decisions promoting their confidence and sense of control. When children have planned what they wish to do they are more engaged in their play, their concentration levels increase and their play becomes increasingly more complex. During planning time adults support the children by listening to them, providing materials to make it an interesting time, and by conversing with them using both language and non-verbal communication techniques.

Work (do) time

Work (do) time starts as soon as planning is complete. Some children will wait until all the children in the group have planned but some will need to be allowed to go off to begin their work time as soon as they finish planning. Work time is such an important part of the High/Scope approach as it allows the children to be in control of what they do, to build up social relations with other children, to develop initiative, to solve problems and to use language to communicate with others.

During work time children are busy and actively involved with their environment; whatever they plan to do, it is up to them to decide how long they play there. In all settings at work time you may have children staying in one area or playing with one thing for the whole of work time as well as children who spend a short time in lots of areas or with many play things. With consistent exposure to plan-do-review, children who flit from one activity to another soon settle when they realise the equipment will always be there for them to use when they want it. During work time children are able to follow through their plans, play with purpose, try out new ideas and construct their knowledge.

Practitioners in a High/Scope setting are very involved in the children's world and throughout work time support the children in their play activities. They use this time to find out what children are interested in and generate ideas for small group times. They observe children at play and the observations are noted and later recorded on the child's observation record. Throughout work time the practitioner is available to the children, offering comfort if it is needed, joining in with the play, talking with the children and supporting them to resolve conflict. Work

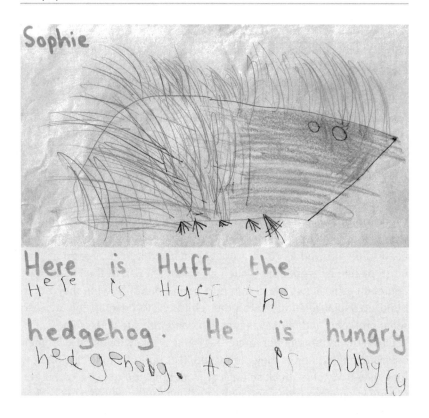

Sophie

Here is Huff the
hedgehog. He is hungry

time is not seen as a time when the children are busy so the adults can get on with something else; the adults' role within work time is vital. In supporting children through their work time we give them the message that their plans, thoughts and actions are valuable to us and we enjoy spending time with them.

It is, however, the adult's role to bring work time to an end and practitioners will use a signal, a tambourine maybe, to indicate that there are five minutes left of work time before tidy-up time. This allows the children to finish off what they are doing and lessens the feelings and frustrations often seen in young children when they are asked to stop something that they are enjoying. After all how many of us adults would appreciate someone suddenly telling us to stop what we were doing when we were having a good time. Tidy-up time can be signalled by again the tambourine or maybe a tidy-up song; this turns what is sometimes a difficult time in settings into something fun.

In a High/Scope setting tidy-up time is seen as part of work time and a learning opportunity for the children. Children are again supported by the adults and actively begin to put the toys back in the areas, on shelves or in their storage containers. The children are usually very keen to use the brushes and dustpans to sweep up and cloths to wipe the tables.

Visitors to a High/Scope setting often comment on how busy the children are but at the same time how quiet the setting can be. Children who are motivated in their own play, as during plan-do-review time, are fully involved with the activity. This in turn lessens the need for loud voices; we all know how quiet children can become when engrossed in an activity they enjoy.

Review time

At review time (sometimes called recall time as children have to recall what they have been doing) children will meet back with the children and adult they planned with. This is a great chance for children to show anything they have made or a picture that they have drawn or painted. Review time encourages children to remember what they have been doing and gives them the opportunity to put into words their thoughts and actions. It encourages children to associate their plans with their actions and the outcomes of those actions; it also allows the adults to introduce new words into the child's vocabulary, thus supporting and expanding their knowledge. Children are encouraged to talk about not only what they have done but how they did it, thinking through problems they encountered and how they were solved. They can, and often do, ask each other questions about what they have been doing, for example, 'What is that?' 'How does that work?' 'What did you eat in the home corner?' By giving children this opportunity to talk about what they have been doing the High/Scope approach again fosters children's self-esteem, confidence and language development in a natural way.

At review time practitioners may use some of the same planning strategies outlined previously. This again supports the children to link their plans through play to review.

> When children recall their work time experiences, they form a mental version of their experience based on their ability to understand and interpret what they have done.
>
> Hohmann and Weikart 2002: 225)

Choice time

With the youngest children plan-do-review is not formally used as such; however, in a High/Scope setting choice time is substituted. In this time a practitioner working with this age range would commentate on the babies' play and interact as necessary. The practitioner would offer a variety of materials for the youngest children to choose from and using their voice, eye contact and expressions, follow the babies' lead. With the older toddler a small selection of photographs (two or three) of toys or equipment may be used to support the toddlers' emerging ability to make their own selection.

A balance between interaction and sitting back and allowing the babies to explore the materials of choice supports them to learn, develop and have fun together.

> Choice time is a sustained block of time when infants and toddlers can investigate and explore materials and actions ... In a supportive and safe environment that affords interesting materials and opportunities as well as space to move in various ways, each child chooses what to do based on personal interest, inclinations and level of development.
>
> (Post and Hohmann 2000: 247)

Snack time

As in all good settings snack time is seen as more than just an opportunity for children to have some refreshment. In a High/Scope setting the children come together in small groups with an adult, sometimes the key worker and his/her children but not always. The children and adult meet around a table and children take on roles like handing out the cups and plates. The children are offered a drink of milk, water or juice and this is often in small jugs so the children can pour their own drink. A healthy snack of seasonal fruit is offered to the children by one of their peers. Children enjoy taking on roles at this time; it boosts their self-esteem but also cements them as a community of friends who share what they have.

At snack time the children are free to talk with their friends or the adult present, or to just sit and think about their next adventure. Children are often keen to talk about what they have been doing at work time and review can often spill over into snack time.

Some settings may choose not to have a set snack time but instead have it on offer throughout the session in a special area. Children are then free to decide when they have their snack. This can be seen as sharing control with the children, giving them the choice as to when they have a snack, although some practitioners feel the opportunity to meet together in a small group, to join in with conversation and develop language skills and have a shared experience is lost. Individual teams must decide for themselves what they feel is best for their setting and the children in their care.

Large-group time

The session will end with a large-group time when a story and/or some singing may occur. It is valuable to the children to come back as a large group; they may like to share something they have done at work time, a picture or model for example, or share some achievement. It also reinforces for the children the sense of belonging to the group setting. As this segment is at the end of the session the children are often ready for their parents/carers to collect and are keen to share the events of the session with them.

A High/Scope setting is a busy, creative and supportive environment for young children's learning. The setting is advantageous to children's active learning and fosters their interests and ideas. Materials available to the children support their learning but also extend their thinking and experiences. They are appropriately stored and accessible to both children and adults.

The High/Scope routine is consistent, giving children a sense of security and control in the knowledge of what happens next. At the same time it is flexible, allowing for unplanned for events to be included and enjoyed.

> In a High/Scope early childhood setting adults create a child-centered environment. Children have space in which to work with materials they choose based on their personal interests and initiatives.
>
> (Hohmann and Weikart 2002: 149)

3 Resources

In a High/Scope setting practical resources such as equipment will be much the same as any other early years setting's but with some subtle differences and additions. In this chapter we will look at the resources available to the practitioner in the setting. This includes a range of manufactured play equipment and natural materials alongside 'real' objects and equipment.

In a High/Scope setting resources also include the adults themselves who work with the children and the way in which they interact together. Practitioners also have the key developmental indicators that they use to guide them in their observations of the children in the setting. Some settings may use the Child Observation Records (CORs) in which they record their observations.

Practical resources

A High/Scope setting will have a variety of manmade equipment available to the children as well as natural and 'real' objects. Let's look at the areas in turn and what you may find in there.

Block/construction area

At some stage all children will spend some time in the block area. From exploring the shapes, textures and weight the children begin to line them up, stack them, put them into other boxes and empty them out again. Their play then develops on to building structures where they will consider balance and height; they will also combine them with other materials such as cars, animals and people and build garages, roads, enclosures and houses.

The block area should provide a range of blocks in all shapes, sizes and colours, wooden and plastic blocks, planks of wood and cardboard boxes that children can use to build structures with. You will also find smaller construction materials such as Duplo, Lego, Mobilo and Stickle Bricks for their smaller construction projects. If space allows it's good to have nearby some alternative building materials that can be easily combined to extend the children's play, for example blankets or material, rope, carpet squares and large cardboard tubes. Children love to build and will use the open-ended materials practitioners supply in a never-ending range of ways.

For example, children in the nursery had made a square of large blocks on the floor and were collecting the wild animals from the small-world play. 'Look, we're making a zoo,' said one child. 'We need a roof,' said another and went off to collect something suitable. He came back with the old shower curtain that had been used the day before when they had

had fun with paint. 'This will be ok, and we can see what the animals are doing,' he said proudly. As this example shows, children soon become confident not only in their own ability but in the creative ways in which materials can be used.

Art/craft area

The art area can be used by children in several ways; some children just like to explore the materials, the feel of the glue or the sound paper makes when you tear it, for example. Others will want to make something special or specific, like a painting for a parent or a birthday card. An area stocked with a wide range of materials would support both these types of play and exploration.

In the art area you will find: a wide range of paper in various shapes and sizes, lined, plain and checked; a selection of pens, pencils and crayons in various thicknesses; paint in a rainbow of colours and brushes from very fine through to household size; and rulers, rubbers and hole punches for children to try out and use. You will also find craft equipment such as glue (various types), material, scraps of paper, magazines, pictures, newspapers, old wallpaper, ribbon, wool, scissors (various sizes and cutting edges), staplers, sticky tape, cardboard tubes and other 'junk' boxes – again the list is endless.

As this area is quite high on consumable materials it's a good idea to think about what could be recycled; providing old envelopes, junk mail, computer paper (with one blank side) and old calendars can help. It's also a good idea to look at the community the setting is in to see if there are any factories or large offices that may throw out equipment that could have a play value for the children. Or use the local scrap store if you have one, these are great places for stocking the art area.

Jenny, aged 4 years, collected an old diary from the art area (the setting had been given various sized, unused diaries from a local company where one of the parents worked). 'My Dad has one of these, he uses it for work,' she said. Jenny then sat at a table and wrote in the diary, 'I need a phone 'cus I need to make some appointments.' Jenny went over to the house area and collected a telephone, she 'phoned' several people speaking on the phone and writing in the diary. This use of a 'throwaway' item really supported Jenny in her play and her re-enactment of what she had seen her Dad do.

Water and sand area

From infancy children love to play with both water and sand. These natural elements hold fascination and the opportunity to use and manipulate them as children wish. Children are free to pour, splash, stir, mix, build, fill and empty on their own or with friends. Sand and water trays can be bought as free-standing pieces of furniture but if space is limited or the setting runs from a shared space, washing up bowls or baby baths can be excellent substitutes. Outdoor sand boxes or pits can be great for group play and allow for children to use more of their larger muscles. Inside sand and water trays or boxes will be housed alongside the equipment available for the children to use. This can be man-made boats, funnels, jugs etc. in the water and spades, buckets, rakes etc. in the sand tray.

In a High/Scope setting you may also see other equipment such as tubes, sponges, corks, colanders, squeezy bottles, animals, shells, fir cones and stones that can be used in both the sand and water trays as well as in other areas of the setting. This equipment can be stored in see-through boxes or old vegetable racks are great; children are able to see what is available and make their own choices. Nearby will always be suitable aprons, dustpans and brushes to aid sweeping the sand and mops for the water.

In High/Scope settings you may also find alternatives to sand and water in these areas, such as wood shavings, snow, gravel, leaves and even shaving foam.

For example, practitioners in a High/Scope nursery had spent time making ice cubes for the children and one morning had put them in the water tray. On discovery of the ice cubes the children spent a long time exploring them, finding out what happened when they were held and how cold they were. The language that was used by the children was varied and included cold, drippy, wet, melted, white, hard, slippy and gone!

House area

In many early years settings this area is more commonly called the role-play area. In a High/Scope setting role play can happen wherever the children choose it to: for example, if the children wish to dress up as firemen and then go into the block area to build their fire engine this would be supported. Children's desire to imitate the world and people around them is so strong that the value in having a house area available at all times should not be denied them.

Children can spend a lot of time in the house area; the space and time to explore the equipment and to use their imagination to enter another world is invaluable. The house area allows children to make sense of the world around them, as they can explore feelings and re-enact events in their lives in a comfortable and safe setting. The opportunities to play with others are many so children learn to cooperate and communicate with their peers.

The house area should be equipped with child-sized furniture as this is made so that children can use it comfortably and safely; however, it can be stocked with real, adult-sized utensils. These are usually more durable and reflect the children's experiences outside of the setting. They also support the children's innate desire to imitate the adults around them; children can be excellent mimics and can be heard and seen on many occasions being Mum, Dad or even a setting practitioner! In a High/Scope setting the house area would contain, as far as possible, equipment that reflects the children's homes: saucepans (various sizes), wok, cutlery, crockery, teapots, sieves, baking tins, washing-up clothes and sponges, a toaster, kettle, iron, microwave, clocks, radio and telephone. The list is endless!

By giving children access to real, life-size objects they can fully involve themselves in role play from their home experiences. Electrical items have great play value and can be made safe for children by cutting off the cables. Travel-size kettles and irons can be more manageable for some of the younger children. Realistic man-made equipment can also be included in the setting such as play food, plastic tea sets, cutlery etc.

In this area you will find the dressing-up equipment and this can also reflect the home cultures of the children attending the setting. Alongside the shirts, trousers, hats and necklaces should be saris (or a long piece of material which could be a sari but would also double up as a cape or blanket), interesting pieces of material, slippers and shoes. Available should be props that children can use to become someone else, for example stethoscope and bandages to be a doctor or nurse or Wellington boots, a hose and yellow hat to be a fireman. Providing clothes, hats, shoes and bags allows the children to enter each other's world and try out being someone else.

Dolls, male and female, complete with clothes, cots and feeding equipment can also be found in the home area, again allowing children the opportunity to act out their home experiences and to experience being someone else. Other homely additions could be a picture on the wall, plants, cookbooks and photographs.

Items for the house area can often be resourced from a range of places including jumble sales, car boot sales and the children's parents. Asking parents can make them feel included in the setting and they may even volunteer to come into the setting and talk to the children about their clothes, cooking utensils or job role.

mummy with Spider fingers

Small-world play and toy area

In this area the children will play simple games and puzzles, they will repeat their actions and consolidate their learning. Children spend lots of time putting things together and then taking them apart, they fill things and empty them, and they sort and match. To offer the opportunity to do these things this area will contain farm sets, the garage, cars, play people, beads, buttons, puppets, train sets, puzzles, stacking cups or rings and a small selection of games. Often stored in this area are natural materials that easily combine with the man-made to extend and enhance the children's play – items such as fir cones, leaves, stones, shells and corks. Items that are often considered rubbish can have a play value too; empty film cartons, lids from jars or cans and smaller 'real' items such as nuts and bolts, pegs and magnets. These are open-ended and therefore used by the children in a variety of ways depending on their interests.

Two children in the nursery had chosen to play in the small-world area. Kera had chosen the wild animals and was lining them up in family groups. Joe had taken out the cars and was racing them along the floor. Both then selected some pine cones; Kera decided they were trees and hedges to 'keep the animals in' but as Joe crashed the cars into them he said, 'these are the crash barriers to stop the cars going off the track.'

Book corner

The book corner is usually a cosy, quiet space for children to use. They like to look at the books alone, with friends or have an adult read a favourite story to them. The book corner should be friendly and welcoming and have some comfy cushions and if space, an arm chair. It's here the children's interest in language and early reading from picture reading through letter recognition to 'reading' a favourite story is fostered. This area should contain bought books containing stories (some with only pictures and some with pictures and words), poems, songs and rhymes. Other 'reading' material should be included such as magazines, notepads and brochures. Having story props, like puppets for example, so children can re-enact their favourite story with friends, extends the experience of reading for young children.

Including books that the children have made, for example recording an event at the setting or a day trip, and photograph albums can prove very popular. Children enjoy recalling and retelling events they have experience of and books of this sort support these skills in young children. Using photographs also allows children to share themselves and possibly their families with others. Children love words and language so having material that reflects the languages of your community is a good idea but you should always have examples of other languages and cultures for children to experience. If space allows having some writing equipment available to the children to create their own books is a good idea, or the book corner could be sited next to the art and/or computer to allow for free flow of the use of the materials for the children to follow their interests.

Amy, aged 4 years, had been attending the High/Scope setting since she was 2 years old. At planning time Amy chose to read books, and Nicky asked if she would like to do it alone or with someone. Amy responded, 'I shall read to myself then I can use the words I like.'

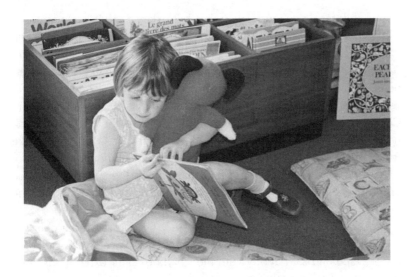

Technology and computer area

As children are growing up in an ever more technological age the addition of a computer may be something settings have. Thought must be given to the programs that the children will have access to and there are many specifically designed for young children on the market today. Programmes that allow children to draw, compare, match and count are often favourites as well as games that allow two children to play together. Children using this area will need the hardware – computer, monitor, keyboard, mouse and printer if it is affordable – as well as appropriate seating and desk space.

Children who experience success at the computer will often, by their enthusiasm, attract others to join them in the computer activity. Anxious to demonstrate their expertise, these 'expert' children may offer to help other, more reticent children to use the computer.

(Hohmann and Weikart 2002: 142)

Music and movement area

Young children enjoy music; they sing, hum, dance and listen to music as well as play and explore instruments. Here you will find a variety of made instruments but also equipment that children could use to make their own sounds, for example drums, tambourines, shakers, triangles, xylophones, bells, maracas, recorders, whistles and simple blocks. Children love to listen to music, so a simple tape/CD recorder they can use with tapes and CDs from around the world is a great thing to offer them. Having some headphones available can help with the noise levels. Children also like to record themselves so having this facility on the equipment is fun too.

As it's a movement area materials that support the children to dance and move such as scarves, ribbons, small balls and hoops should be available too.

On a visit to a local High/Scope nursery I witnessed three children who had planned at work time to use the tape players. One selected a story tape and sat happily with the storybook after expertly inserting the correct tape and putting on some headphones, whilst the other two selected a music tape of African drumming and danced around together. All three children were confident in their ability to use the equipment and thoroughly enjoyed the experience.

Woodworking area

As in the home area, children really enjoy being able to use 'real' materials and equipment they see the adults in the world around them using.

Some can spend lengths of time just sawing or knocking nails into a block of wood, while other children will wish to make something such as a boat or walkie-talkie. This area can sometimes be incorporated into the art area or at least sited near it to allow the children to paint what they have made or to use materials from the art area to adorn their creation.

Items in the woodworking area would include hammers, saws, screwdrivers, nails, screws, pliers, clamps, nuts, bolts, wood scraps, dowelling and safety goggles. Practitioners often worry about using these materials with children but with supervision children can be very careful and as in all the areas any issues are seen as opportunities to problem solve.

Play space for under 2s

When working with the under 2s in a High/Scope setting the play spaces are not so defined into areas. Infants and toddlers need more space to be free to move about and develop through their physical body. Resources are still evident within the space and would offer the infants and toddlers appropriate materials to explore, manipulate and interact with.

This variety of equipment is stored within the room, often on the floor, to aid the older babies to self select at choice time. The equipment would also be grouped, for example blocks all together, treasure baskets and book baskets. Use of sturdy low shelving around the walls to aid storage and maybe divide quiet play space from the busier play is useful; this also supports a flexible use of the room. Often in the under 2s environment a place for a large comfy chair or sofa, if space allows, can be a great addition. This allows practitioners somewhere to comfort distressed infants, read stories in a cosy way and be relaxed and comfortable when feeding a baby its bottle. It also allows the infants and toddlers themselves somewhere to relax and take time out and gives the room a more homely feel, which is important in helping the infants and toddlers when settling into day care.

Outdoor area

Children love to be outside, to explore and have the opportunity to climb, run, skip, ride bikes and do the things that we adults are not able to let them do inside. Having the opportunity to be outside every day is essential for the growth and development of young children; they are able to explore the natural world, listen to the sounds, smell the smells and feel the textures of the world around them. Children are often able to demonstrate different skills or sides to their individual character in the outdoor area. Having the opportunity to use their larger muscles enables them to show their skills at climbing or balancing, something they are not always able to do inside.

Within the Childcare Act of 2006 the British Government set out that all childcare settings have a legal responsibility to ensure that children in their care have access to stimulating and challenging outdoor play space by 2008. Practitioners who work with young children need to ensure that the outdoor environment is as valued and important to the children's well-being and development as the indoors. Access to the outdoor space should, if at all possible, be available to children simultaneously with indoor activities.

High/Scope considers the outdoor space as of equal value to the indoor learning environment. Throughout the daily routine children should have access to the outdoor space: they can experience many opportunities for active learning through exploration and interaction in the outdoor learning environment. Outdoor play spaces need to have a variety of learning zones for children to explore and experience.

- **Transition zone** – this is the area immediately outside the setting building. It is where children can spend anything from a few seconds to a few minutes having a look around the outdoor space and considering what they would like to do.

- **Manipulative or creative zone** – where children are able to develop their fine motor skills. This may include equipment that can be easily transported from the indoors, for example puzzles, small blocks and beads and/or paints, clay and natural materials. This area may have a sand tray which may contain an alternative to sand such as rice, sawdust or other tactile material.

- **Fantasy zone** – through being offered equipment such as play people and animals, children are able to develop their imaginative play in a stimulating way.

- **Social zone** – this is where children and practitioners can meet to share what they have been doing, talk together or just watch the other children at play. This can easily be achieved by the addition of a picnic table or bench.

- **Dramatic zone** – as its name suggests this is an area for role play. Children can have opportunities to try out other roles, for example in a fire station or garage, or with the addition of a tent experience a taste of camping.

- **Physical zone** – in this area the children get the opportunity to use their large muscles and develop their gross motor skills. This zone should be big enough for children to run around and also provide children with the opportunity to take risks such as climbing, jumping, balancing and swinging. Paths or walkways can provide space for bikes and wheeled toys. This area may contain fixed equipment such as swings and slides (if space allows) but also equipment that children can choose from such as tunnels, bean bags, hoops and bats and balls.

- **Natural zone or gardening area** – this is where children can have the opportunity to dig and play with mud. The chance to grow flowers and vegetables presents itself too. Children's opportunities to link with the natural world are often limited so by offering this experience we support their knowledge and understanding of nature.

Infants and toddlers also need access, where possible, to some outside space. This not only allows them to explore a different medium such as the grass but develop even further physically. The benefits to all children of spending some time outside in the fresh air most days to aid sleep and eating are well known.

The area used by the under 2s should include some simple physical structures to support their emerging control over their bodies and also some shady areas for relaxation and play. A variety of textures and floor coverings can be beneficial, for example grass, decking, concrete and mud as at this age children learn through their senses and this supports that development.

Practitioners in settings with no outdoor space need to think creatively to be able to offer the children outdoor experiences. No matter how large

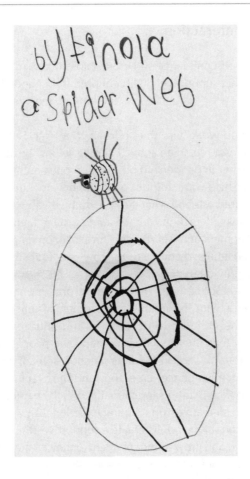

by Finola

a Spider Web

an indoor space it cannot replace the sights, sounds and smells of being outside. A local park nearby is a good alternative and the walk to the park should be seen as part of the experience. Whilst enjoying the walk lots of conversation can take place about what the children and practitioners are seeing, who they meet, shops or buildings they pass and the street environment they walk along. In the park the children can spend time exploring the trees and shrubs, play large-group games or just revel in the open space. This experience is so valuable for children when we consider they may live in flats or houses with limited outdoor space.

Adult–child interaction

> Children's self-confidence and friendships flourish in a setting where adults interact supportively with children throughout the day.
>
> (Hohmann and Weikart 2002: 42)

Practitioners who work with the children in a High/Scope setting are seen as a great resource. In an active learning setting the adults and children work together in partnership building on one another's interests. In forming partnerships with children practitioners are letting the children know that their interests and what they are doing is valued. From the very beginning positive interaction with the adults around them is essential for a child's development and well-being. From the moment we are born we need supportive adults to enable us to grow and flourish into confident, well-rounded individuals.

Within a High/Scope early years setting practitioners form strong supportive bonds with the infants and toddlers. Their primary role is to encourage the children to develop in an unhurried way through interaction with toys, their environment and the people around them. They become the infants and toddlers' anchor, someone they can rely on for reassurance, guidance, care and fun. The practitioners become very tuned in to the children's individuality which enables them to offer security as well as creative, fun learning experiences.

In a High/Scope setting adults create a supportive climate for children to learn, have fun and grow in independence; they create a well-ordered environment that supports children's interests and a consistent routine in which children can feel secure. Through active learning experiences children are able to make choices and decisions supported by the practitioners. High/Scope practitioners work in partnership with children, they encourage and assist them in their play and support them to solve problems they may encounter along the way. High/Scope believes children thrive when immersed in a supportive climate:

> [I]t enables them to focus on their own interests and initiatives, try out their ideas, talk about their actions, and solve child-sized problems in age appropriate ways ... it stimulates and strengthens

children's ongoing development of trust, autonomy, initiative, empathy and self-confidence.

(Hohmann and Weikart 2002: 49)

High/Scope believes there are five key elements to creating a supportive climate for children's learning:

1. Shared control between children and adults

When adults and children share control they build a mutual relationship that acknowledges trust and respect for each other. Practitioners share control with children by taking cues from their play; in this way the children stay in control and the adult assists the play. Practitioners participate with children's play on their terms; they refrain from leading the play but follow the individual child's ideas, thoughts and rules. They learn from the children's exploration and discoveries.

2. A focus on children's strengths

By using observations of the children High/Scope practitioners can incorporate the children's interests into the setting. By looking at what the children can do adults use the child's own motivation to extend their learning and understanding. They also use these observations to plan activities for children that are of interest to them, thus building on their strengths and interests.

3. Forming authentic relationships with children

High/Scope practitioners share themselves with the children in their care. By being themselves, sharing their own unique strengths, interests, skills and enthusiasm, children's experiences are enriched. In this way they build real relationships with children on a mutual footing through conversation and shared experiences.

4. A commitment to support children's play

Play is what children do naturally; it's fun, creative, enjoyable and rewarding. It is the child's 'work' and where they feel in control of themselves and the world around them. Play is how children learn and find out about the world around them. By using the ingredients of active learning – materials, manipulation, choice, language and support – adults in a High/Scope setting sustain children's play. They value it as a means of constructing knowledge and understanding for children and as a vehicle for interaction with those around us.

5. **Adopting a problem-solving approach to conflict**

When working with young children conflict is inevitable; quite naturally children are egocentric and have only their personal needs in mind. High/Scope practitioners see conflict as opportunities for children to develop skills in problem solving and concentrate on enabling children to resolve the issues rather than using punishment. (The High/Scope problem-solving approach to conflict will be looked at more fully later in this chapter.)

Encouragement

In a High/Scope setting the practitioners will use encouragement with young children rather than praise. This is something that some people find hard to grasp as we live in a society where praise for a job well done or for doing something right is seen as the norm. For example we have all experienced a 'well done' or a 'good boy/girl' and probably felt OK about it, but how much better would we have felt if the person saying 'well done' had actually said, 'you worked really hard on that picture' or 'your story is really exciting, I like the bit where the dog jumps into the sea'? In that way we understand what it is we have done well as the specific action is acknowledged.

Although children seem to crave praise from the adults around them, in the long term children (and adults) begin to act and behave in a way they think the adults want them to. They conform to another's rules, making them dependent on the adults for the praise. This can have a negative impact on children, for example it can stop children evaluating their own work leading to a decrease in self-esteem and worth. It can cause anger and frustration between children who perceive others are getting more praise then themselves and this can lead to conformity to the adult's rules just to receive the praise. In the long term this can lead to children becoming demotivated, discouraged from having a go at things and so increase their dependence on the adults around them. These are not traits the High/Scope approach supports and nurtures in children or adults.

In High/Scope settings practitioners use encouragement as an alternative to praise. Encouragement is specific and can focus on the process rather than the end product. We know that for children often the 'doing' is far more important than having something to show for it at the end. For example, a child may spend some time exploring materials:

At small group time Molly (22 months) spent 20 minutes putting glue onto a spatula and watching it drip onto a piece of paper with one hand and with the other she explored the feel of the glue between her fingers. When this was noticed by the practitioner she said, 'Molly you've made a puddle with your glue.' The practitioner accepted that Molly was happy with exploring the glue and was descriptive and specific about what she had done.

Encouragement is personal, it is specific to the child therefore avoids comparisons and competition between children. Practitioners will play alongside children and encourage their individual efforts by copying their actions, taking turns with them and generally following their lead. They will encourage children to talk about their 'work' and ideas as this develops their self-esteem, thus making them feel good about what they are doing. Practitioners make this possible by asking open-ended questions such as 'tell me about your picture' or 'How did you build this tower?' These are specific to what each child has done thus supporting them to extend their thinking and language skills.

High/Scope practitioners acknowledge children's work with specific comments; this can be done as they interact with children in play so it becomes a natural part of what they do. These comments are non-judgemental responses to children who seek out an adult's approval or acknowledgement. For example they may say, 'you've built a tall tower with the blue and yellow bricks' rather than 'good tower, Joe' or 'I see you have painted some blue and yellow lines down your paper.'

When practitioners have used/been using praise with children for a long time it is difficult, strange even, to try to use encouragement. But as with all new skills it takes time and practice and quickly shows benefits to the children's self-esteem and well-being.

Problem-solving approach to conflict resolution

When children come together to play and explore the world around them, conflict is sure to follow. In a High/Scope active learning setting conflict situations are seen as an important experience for children to learn from. Practitioners hold in mind that young children are very self-centred and only think of things from their own perspective. They are growing away from adults, seeking out their independence and gaining control of their world and as part of this process they come into conflict with their peers.

High/Scope uses a problem-solving approach that is based on child development and research; included in this are the six steps to conflict resolution, small-group problem-solving and prevention strategies. Let's look at these three areas one by one.

Six steps to conflict resolution

1. Approach calmly and stop any hurtful actions

Adults go to children in a calm manner and stop children hurting each other. Get down to the children's level and use your normal conversational level voice. Reach out to children who seem hurt and allow them to come to you, remembering that not all children will accept physical contact.

2. Acknowledge children's feelings

This is essential; it is believed that without this step the process may fail. By naming children's feelings, 'Sarah you sound angry' or 'Peter you look sad', it not only gives them the words for how they are feeling but it allows children to express themselves fully. This will then enable them to move on to the solution process.

By acknowledging children's feelings it tells the child it is OK to feel that way and safe to do so. As children mature adults may need to reframe some hurtful feelings expressed by the children; for example, a child may say, 'I hate you' which the practitioner can reframe as, 'You're feeling angry about this.'

3. Gather information

This step allows the children involved to tell what has happened. By asking 'What's up?' or 'What's the problem?' the adult gives the children the space to tell their story and listen to the other child's story too. 'What' questions are very concrete; they ask for facts and details and acknowledge the stages of development young children are at.

4. Restate the problem

The practitioner restates simply what they have heard from the children, for example, 'So the problem is you both want the Thomas train.' This helps to clarify the problem and allows for any confusion to be cleared away before solutions can be found. It also allows for children to clarify any misunderstanding on the part of the adult.

5. Ask for ideas for solutions and choose one together

Here the practitioner simply asks, 'What can we do to solve this?' This supports the children to present their own solutions and allows them to stay in control of the problem, seeing themselves as problem solvers. When a solution seems to have been agreed the practitioner would say, 'So the solution is ... Is that OK?' This again checks out that all are happy about the solution. This step can take some time to begin with as solutions are suggested and rejected.

Occasionally the children are not able to come up with a solution so the practitioner can suggest one for consideration as a last result. If this happens remember to offer two solutions, for example, 'Maybe you could share the Thomas train or we could find another one.' This still leaves the children in control as it is up to them to select or reject the proffered solution.

6. Be prepared to give follow-up support

Sometimes solutions need to be clarified when play begins and the practitioner can encourage the children to recognise themselves as problem solvers by saying, 'You solved this problem.' It is sometimes helpful to stay nearby to watch the play begin again; this allows the practitioner to offer any support if it is needed.

As with all new skills these steps to resolving conflict take time and practice to master, both for the practitioner and the children. This process supports children when they need it but allows them to retain control and develop confidence in their own abilities.

Over time, this is a process that children come to trust, one that enriches relationships and promotes increasingly complex thinking.

Mistakes and differences become the catalysts for growth, providing the opportunity for change. The problem-solving approach enables children to handle disputes constructively and creatively as they become independent problem solvers together.

(Evans 2002: 44)

Whilst outside Cameron and Kain frequently wanted to use the 'cosy coupe' car. High/Scope practitioners supported both boys through the conflict resolution process on several occasions very successfully. After a few weeks Cameron said, 'Nicky, look, Kain and me are sharing the car, we worked it out together. He goes round the garden once then we swap over. I go round then swap.' 'You worked it out together so you can both have ago in the car,' Nicky replied. The consistent support from practitioners and handling of this conflict situation gave both boys the skills and confidence to manage on their own. These boys are now able to use these negotiation skills in other areas of their lives.

The problem-solving approach to conflict as described above can also be used with infants and toddlers; however, the practitioner will have to model the solutions and vocalise what is happening. Although infants and toddlers are very egocentric this consistent approach from practitioners supports them to develop their thinking and reasoning skills in the long term. This helps them to feel a sense of control over themselves and their growing interactions with their peers.

With the support of their caregivers, toddlers can develop and practice the ability to solve many of their own social conflicts. Throughout their efforts, they exercise thinking and reasoning skills, gain a sense of control over the solution or outcome of the problem, experience co-operation and develop trust in themselves, their peers and caregivers.

(Post and Hohmann 2000: 90)

Small-group problem solving

This is a good strategy to use when there is a problem that is affecting the whole group. A problem such as running indoors in which children could harm themselves and their friends is a common one. In small-group problem solving the adult facilitates with opportunities for the children to contribute their ideas and thoughts; in this way any solutions are generated and accepted by everyone.

The practitioner would describe the problem in a way that does not single out any child and uses feeling words to convey the concern. For example, 'I'm worried that people will get hurt if we run around indoors' puts the emphasis of concern onto the adult rather than the children's negative behaviour. As with the six steps to conflict resolution the practitioner would ask for ideas on how to solve this issue. Children in the small group are given the opportunity to discuss the issue and share their ideas and solutions to the problem. After each child has had an opportunity to suggest a solution the adult's role is to summarise the ideas given and encourage the group to select one to try.

In my experience this worked very well when a few of the children consistently kicked footballs around the garden, knocking the children on the bikes. After several attempts at individual conflict resolution the practitioners decided to try group problem solving. The group gathered on the carpet and the practitioner said, 'I am worried that people are getting hurt in the garden, we need to find a way to play safely.' The children were quick to respond with 'Yeah, it really hurts' and 'It's not nice, it makes me cry.' The practitioner acknowledged these statements and asked, 'Well, what shall we do about this?' The children were eager to offer solutions and came up with 'We could not have balls anymore' and 'We should only have footballs on some days.' These solutions were quickly dismissed by some of the children as unfair to those children who enjoyed playing with the footballs. 'We could build a fence to stop the balls.' The practitioner agreed this sounded a good idea but might cost lots of money. Lots of discussion ensued about how to raise money to pay for things you might need. After some time the practitioner brought the discussion back by restating the problem and the children came up with the idea of only playing football on the bottom level of the garden and allowing the bikes only at the top level. All seemed happy with this solution and the children could be heard for quite a long time after reminding each other to keep the balls in the lower half of the garden.

Group problem solving supports children to work collaboratively on an issue that affects them all to some extent. It supports their developing cooperation skills and decisions made by children are more likely to be upheld by them. This way of dealing with social conflict can be an enjoyable experience for all:

> Those involved can relax into the thoughtful give and take of finding a solution that works for everyone. Children can be surprisingly insightful during these discussions, offering solutions that reflect their unique thinking and generous natures.
>
> (Evans 2002: 286)

Prevention strategies

In any setting practitioners endeavour to ensure all children have a fun and happy time and when conflict arises can wonder if anything could have been done to prevent it. High/Scope does not believe that conflict should be avoided as it teaches children vital skills in communication and negotiation but there are ways to support its reduction. The strategies listed below give children a sense of control over their play and environment and security in the routine and adults who support them. As a result fewer conflicts arise, making for a more supportive and emotionally balanced environment for young children where they feel safe, valued and encouraged.

- Maintain limits and expectations for behaviour that are developmentally appropriate.

- Provide many choices for play – plentiful materials and easy storage.

- Establish and follow a consistent daily routine – use pictures if necessary.

- Model respectful ways of interacting with others and using materials.
- Plan for transitions – keep them short and fun.

(Hohmann and Weikart 2002: 404–5)

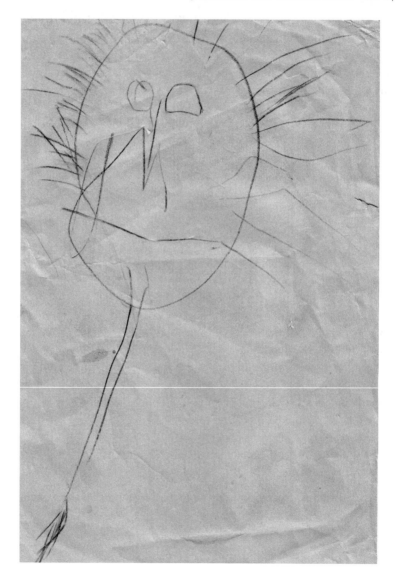

Key developmental indicators

Throughout their time in a High/Scope setting young children are encouraged to make choices about what they do. They interact with both adults and children asking questions, solving problems and developing knowledge. In this active learning environment children are engaging in the key developmental indicators.

> The High/Scope pre-school key experiences *[now key developmental indicators]* are a series of statements describing the social, cognitive and physical development of children aged 2½ to 5. The key *[developmental indicators]* describe what young children do, how they perceive their world and the kinds of experiences that are important for their development.
> (Hohmann and Weikart 2002: 297)

Key developmental indicators are High/Scope's foundation for children's learning and have been developed using research within the USA giving greater weight to child development and problem solving. High/Scope UK now use these in its practice as it supports all the development within early years education and the introduction of the Early Years Foundation Stage (EYFS). The key developmental indicators encompass all aspects of the EYFS and continue to support practitioners in their work with young children. High/Scope practitioners in the UK now use key developmental indicators as building blocks of thinking and reasoning of children's development.

The key developmental indicators are divided into five content areas:

- Approaches to learning

- Language, literacy and communication

- Social and emotional development

- Physical development, health and well-being

- Arts and science.

The arts and science area is subdivided into: mathematics, which incorporates seriation, number and space; science and technology incorporating classification and time; social studies and the arts, which incorporates visual art, dramatic art and music.

High/Scope practitioners use the key developmental indicators to guide them in their work with young children and keep them in mind when observing and planning activities for young children. High/Scope believes these indicators are 'key' in that they are vital to children's development of knowledge; they also offer choices for the child and can be repeated many times. For example, under the science and technology – classification heading is the sorting and matching key developmental indicator: a young child may sort and match bricks in the block area by size or colour, then move onto the house area and match the cups to their saucers and then go on to the art area and after drawing match all the pens to their correct colour lids. This child is repeatedly sorting and matching but uses different objects and materials to construct and develop his knowledge and understanding.

Key developmental indicators are seen as learning opportunities for children and practitioners would use their knowledge of individual children, built up through observations, to plan appropriate activities for children's needs. For example, after observing the child above who has sorted and matched items throughout work time in the setting, the practitioner may plan a small-group time around sorting and matching. He/she may offer the children a collection of bricks in several colours and shapes for each of them in a box. The practitioner may ask the children to see if they can make two things with the bricks that are the same. Some children may just play with the bricks building towers and knocking them down again, but some will create shapes with them that match in colour and design. The practitioner would support the children by describing what he/she sees the children doing and using the bricks in the same way as the children.

> Activities must be able to accommodate children's different abilities, as well as their different preferences. This need for flexibility lies at the heart of the idea of key *[developmental indicators]*.
>
> (Hohmann and Weikart 2002: 297)

When working with young children the practitioner would be observing their play and development and using this knowledge to write anecdotal evidence of what the children can do. These anecdotes are then linked to the key developmental indicators on each individual child's observation record.

The complete list of key developmental indicators can be found in the Appendix and provides a composite picture of children's development.

High/Scope Preschool Child Observation Records

As in all early years settings a record of the children's development must be kept and shared with the parents/carers at regular intervals. High/Scope has developed the preschool Child Observation Record (COR) as a tool for practitioners to use, which some settings use but not all. In the COR the practitioners can record their observations of children thus providing a useful and accurate picture of an individual child's development and abilities.

Throughout a session in a High/Scope setting the practitioner would be interacting with the children but also observing their learning and listening to their conversation. Practitioners make anecdotal notes about children as they play during a session, therefore recording what children do naturally. These anecdotes can be written in a small notebook or on a piece of paper that can, at a later time, be transferred onto the COR or any record of the children's development that is being used by the setting. This takes away the need to separate children to carry out an assessment which can sometimes give a false response. Anyone involved with the children can write an anecdote about that child to be included on the COR; this includes parents/carers as well as other staff such as cooks and lunchtime staff. Anecdotes must include not only what happened but also the child's name and the date. Other evidence of children's development such as drawings, photographs and writing can also be included.

The COR is usually completed and shared with parents three times throughout the school year, at the beginning (or when a child first starts at the setting), halfway through the year and again at the end. The High/Scope practitioner would spend some time each week transferring their

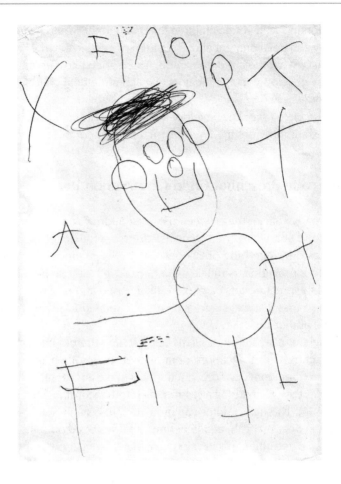

anecdotes onto the children's COR in readiness for sharing with the parents/carers. Although High/Scope settings usually have a key worker system (where a member of staff is responsible for a number of children, including making a link with their family and supporting them to settle into the setting, completing their records and being a point of contact for the child), any member of staff can make anecdotes about any child. The COR provides a comprehensive record of an individual child's ability that can inform and support that child's move on into schooling.

Young children in our care deserve the best we can offer. This includes not only a diverse, ever-changing range of toys and equipment to interact with and learn from but also interesting and interested adults who share themselves in an open and honest way. Practitioners who work with young children also need resources that support them to carry out their role in young children's lives in a comprehensive but flexible way.

As you can see, a High/Scope setting can be resourced with a huge range and diversity of things. Creative thinking around what to include and what to reserve for a later date is down to the team working directly with the children and the children's interests at the time. High/Scope practitioners use their knowledge of what children at a developmental level need to extend their learning, but also use their interactions with the children in their care. This informs them of their interests and what maybe useful to enhance the children's understanding and knowledge. Sharing something about yourself with children can be fun; for example a skill in playing an instrument or even creative storytelling can support children's enjoyment of being in your setting.

The key developmental indicators and the use of CORs support the practitioner to observe children in an organised but flexible way. The key developmental indicators are, as their name suggests, 'key' in the individual child's development of knowledge and 'indicators' that demonstrate children's experiences that they have freely chosen and repeated at will. The knowledge gained from the observations is put to good use in planning meaningful opportunities throughout the setting's daily routine for young children. The COR forms a valuable tool for sharing the children's developing knowledge and interests with parents/carers and the educational environment the child will move onto. This supports the children on their journey into formal education.

4 High/Scope with infants and toddlers

When working with the youngest children a High/Scope setting will look and offer very much the same as any good quality provider. The space for infants and toddlers will be open and adaptable, warm and friendly. The practitioners will be consistent and the daily routine flexible, to suit individual children, but predictable to offer security in what's happening next.

High/Scope with infants and toddlers has its own wheel of learning that reflects the needs of the youngest children and supports practitioners when using the approach within the setting. In the UK the addition of the 'tyre' acknowledges the key role of the family and the evidence-based research available.

Let's look at each of the five segments in turn and how they support practitioners in their work with infants and toddlers.

Active learning

Infants and toddlers are active learners from birth. Even the newborn baby learns very quickly that when it cries an adult will respond; it's learnt that an action creates a response that meets its needs. As active learners infants and toddlers interact with the people and objects around them that grab their attention and interest. Through sounds, gestures and ultimately words they begin to communicate and respond to people and events within their environment. They quickly build trust in those people and environments that enables them to explore physically, with the knowledge and security that their parents and/or practitioners will be there.

In creating an active learning environment for infants and toddlers the practitioners need to consider the whole child and have regard for their physical needs for food, sleep, movement and bodily care; their developmental needs in opportunities to make choices, explore, discover and challenge themselves; and their language needs to communicate, make noises and be responded to.

The High/Scope Infant and Toddler "Wheel of Learning"

Reproduced with kind permission from High/Scope UK
© 2002 High/Scope UK

Infants and toddlers learn by doing – babies learn that by kicking their feet against the cot their toys/rattles make a noise; older babies learn that by pushing their hands on the ground they can hold their heads up and see more; toddlers learn that by pushing a ball into the top of a toy they can watch it roll down and come out the end. All these actions are repeated because they are enjoyable and directed by the child.

They learn with and through their whole body using all their senses, building a bank of knowledge from their actions. They happily gaze at faces and colour-contrast pictures, find their fingers and toes fascinating, babble at movement around them, often cry when they hear another child cry, begin to crawl and pull themselves up. All are actions learnt from doing; a practitioner can support this learning by offering opportunities but cannot teach a child this learning.

We have all witnessed the learning that a young baby goes through when it discovers its own feet or hands, the frowns on its face as the foot or hand comes into focus, the way it immediately plays with the fingers or toes, feeling the skin and then guiding the foot or hand into its mouth for further exploration. The baby has to do this for itself – we cannot teach the sensations and learning that is going on for the individual. The baby is experiencing active learning for itself; it instinctively does it. What it learns from its own fingers it can use to understand its parents' hands, its toys and its food. This way of learning is natural and instinctive and continues throughout our lives and is the core of the High/Scope approach.

Within a High/Scope setting infants and toddlers will be given experiences and stimuli that exploit this natural way of learning through offering all the ingredients of active learning:

Materials – a plentiful supply of interesting objects (ensuring their safety and suitability for very young children) including

- everyday objects – pots, pans, spoons, boxes, paper, bowls

- natural/wooden materials – stones, shells, spoons, bowls cars, rings, material pieces, scarves

- tools – brushes, mops, balloon whisks, spatulas

- messy items – water, soap, playdough, clay, paint

- large, heavy items – big blocks, boxes

- smaller items – Duplo, large buttons, toy cars, pasta, plastic blocks.

Manipulation – offering opportunities to and allowing infants and toddlers to explore and work with the materials in their own way, remembering that they will use their whole body to explore things.

Choice – giving infants and toddlers the choice to select their own materials and how they use them. By having several things in baskets or boxes infants and toddlers can select their own items to explore.

Language – from the infant and toddler. They will babble and attempt simple words that when reflected back by the practitioner will support them to integrate this new knowledge and build relationships with others.

Support – from the adults. Adults support the infants and toddlers' efforts by holding a 'running commentary' about what they see the young children doing. The practitioner will join in with their play and support them to solve problems they may encounter.

By using the five ingredients above throughout the day with infants and toddlers in their play experiences we support their voyage of discovery and learning and have fun together along the way too.

Key experiences

The key experiences form a framework for the early learning and development of infants and toddlers. They have been developed from child observations and reflect their emerging knowledge and actions.

Although within a High/Scope setting the key experiences for over 3s have changed to key developmental indicators, when working with the youngest children key experiences remain.

The infant and toddler key experiences cover 10 areas of learning. Let's have a brief look at them in turn.

Sense of self

Through active learning infants and toddlers begin to understand that they are separate from their parents/carers and develop a sense of control over themselves and their world.

Social relations

Through warm and respectful contact and care with and from adults, infants and toddlers learn to trust and be curious. They make attachments to practitioners which gives them the confidence to explore and be part of a social world. They are more able to express themselves and are developing an awareness of others' feelings, for example when an adult smiles at them they will smile back, when hearing another child cry they often cry in response.

Creative representation

Through active learning and their sensory motor explorations infants and toddlers build a bank of experiences and mental 'pictures' that can be drawn on when they have new experiences. These pictures creatively represent the infants and toddlers' developing knowledge and learning.

Movement

Movement is key to infants and toddlers' development and plays a central role in active learning with this age group. Opportunities to move – to roll, pull themselves up, balance and take those first steps are always available to infants and toddlers in a High/Scope setting.

Music

Music can calm the upset infant and stimulate the developing toddler. Practitioners working with infants and toddlers have all enjoyed watching a young child gently bopping away, moving their arms, rocking from one foot to the other showing obvious enjoyment of the music.

Communication and language

This develops rapidly in the infant and toddler, from the immediate cries at birth through babbling emerging words to a command of language that others can understand. Infants and toddlers also communicate through their bodies. They point, smile, use gestures and objects to share experiences with practitioners. They enjoy and share bold pictures, books, simple stories and songs with those around them.

Explore objects

Infants and toddlers use the objects around them to create their knowledge base. By exploring objects using their whole bodies, their hands, eyes, mouths and feet they begin to make sense of themselves and the world around them.

Quantity and number

Through exploring and play infants and toddlers begin to grasp a basic concept of number. Many of us have experienced the infant who calls for 'more' after he's enjoyed some food. He's beginning to understand the idea of quantity and number.

Space

Infants and toddlers develop an awareness of space through their bodies and interaction with others. From the infant in the cot kicking its legs to the toddler confident in running around the garden or park, their understanding of 'their' space expands with their growing competence and sense of self.

Time

For all infants and toddlers time means now! However, they quickly learn thorough experience of familiar repeated events, for example that a hunger cry means food in infants to toddlers hearing water running and knowing it's time for a bath.

Through this short walk through the key experiences for infants and toddlers you can see how High/Scope and the core ethos of active learning supports their developing knowledge and directs them on their own early learning journey.

Let's now have a look at the other segments of the High/Scope infant and toddler wheel of learning.

Adult–child interaction

> When all goes well, a child has the same supportive family throughout childhood and the family grows together over the years. Infant-toddler settings strive to provide children with similar continuity of care.
>
> (Post and Hohmann 2000: 58)

Infants and toddlers need to be cared for and treated with great care and respect from all adults involved in their young lives. Only then can they begin to develop trusting relationships with adults from which they can grow, learn and develop as individuals. This trusting relationship is built through a continuity of care; therefore within a High/Scope setting it is vital for staff who care for the youngest children to be as stable as humanly possible. The practitioners become the infants and toddlers' anchor, someone they can rely on for reassurance, guidance, care and fun. The practitioners become very tuned in to the children's individuality which enables them to offer security as well as creative, fun learning experiences. A key worker system is essential as it allows the relationship with the parents/carers to be formed thus ensuring a good exchange of ongoing information regarding the child.

Within a High/Scope (and any good quality) setting practitioners touch, hold, speak to and play with the infants and toddlers in a warm and friendly manner. When working with infants and toddlers the play and interactions are physical and unhurried. This gives the child a sense of well-being and respect. Practitioners enjoy being with infants and toddlers and the one-to-one play and closeness that is essential with this age group is celebrated. They enjoy a simple game of peekaboo with an infant or songs, rhymes and finger play with a toddler, experiences which are repeated several times a day.

Practitioners 'tune in' to their key infants and toddlers allowing them to be intuitive to individual needs and provide the necessary level of interaction and support especially when the children are upset, tired or unwell.

Interaction between infants and toddlers is supported and encouraged naturally as the numbers cared for together are low. Also as the toddler matures, relationships with other familiar adults within the setting can develop. This supports the child's confidence and self-esteem and expands his/her circle of friends.

Throughout their time in the setting infants and toddlers are encouraged to explore and play. The environment will be planned and set up to ensure all children can access stimulating equipment suitable for the age of the young children. Practitioners encourage the infants and toddlers by using a running commentary approach:

> Sam, aged 10 months, was sitting on the carpet surrounded by pieces of material. His key worker Jo was nearby. As Sam picked up some material Jo commented, 'Oh, Sam, you have the blue material, you've put it on your head.' As Sam pulled the material

> off, Jo said, 'Boo.' A quick impromptu game of peekaboo began
> as Sam was encouraged by Jo to repeat the action.

As infants develop into toddlers they naturally come into conflict with their peers. They have a strong sense of self and the cry of 'mine' can be frequently heard in many settings. As with the older children within a High/Scope setting the six steps to conflict resolution are used:

1. **Approach calmly and stop any hurtful actions**

   Adults go to children in a calm manner and stop children hurting each other. Get down to the children's level and establish gentle contact with each child.

2. **Acknowledge children's feelings**

   This is essential; it is believed that without this step the process may fail. By naming children's feelings, 'Sarah, you sound angry,' or 'Peter, you look sad,' it not only gives them the words for how they are feeling but it allows children to express themselves fully. This will then enable them to move on to the solution process.

3. **Gather information**

   This step allows the children involved to tell what has happened. However, very young children's verbal skills are still forming so the practitioner needs to describe or retell the information she has gathered from her observation. Asking simple questions that require a single word or nod answer works best.

4. **Restate the problem**

   The practitioner restates simply what they have heard from the children, for example, 'So the problem is you both want the pushchair.' This helps to clarify the problem and allows for any confusion to be cleared away before solutions can be found. It also allows for children to clarify any misunderstanding on the part of the adult.

5. Ask for ideas for solutions and choose one together

Here the practitioner simply asks, 'What can we do to solve this?' This supports the children to present their own solutions and allows them to stay in control of the problem, seeing themselves as problem solvers. With toddlers this may be difficult for them; they can often 'act' their solution rather than use words. When a solution seems to have been agreed the practitioner would say, 'So the solution is ... Is that OK?' This again checks out that all are happy about the solution.

Occasionally the children are not able to come up with a solution so the practitioner can suggest one for consideration as a last result. If this happens remember to offer two solutions, for example, 'Maybe you could share the pushchair or we could find another one.' This still leaves the children in control as it is up to them to select or reject the proffered solution.

6. Be prepared to give follow-up support

Sometimes solutions need to be clarified when play begins and the practitioner can encourage the children to recognise themselves as problem solvers by saying, 'You solved this problem.' It is sometimes helpful to stay nearby to watch the play begin again; this allows the practitioner to offer any support if it is needed.

Although infants and toddlers are very egocentric this consistent approach from practitioners supports them to develop their thinking and reasoning skills in the long term. This helps them to feel a sense of control over themselves and their growing interactions with their peers.

With the support of their caregivers, toddlers can develop and practice the ability to solve many of their own social conflicts. Throughout their efforts, they exercise thinking and reasoning skills, gain a sense of control over the solution or outcome of the problem, experience co-operation and develop trust in themselves, their peers and caregivers.

(Post and Hohmann 2000: 90)

The learning environment

> In a High/Scope setting for infants and toddlers caregivers arrange and equip the environment to provide children with a sense of comfort and well-being and at the same time offer ample opportunity for active learning.
>
> (Post and Hohmann 2000: 98)

In a High/Scope active learning environment for infants and toddlers the space is open but cosy, providing opportunities to move about freely and explore but at the same time have quiet relaxing space too. The space allows the infants and toddlers to do what they are able to but also offers experiences that develop and stretch them, with practitioners who enjoy their company.

Materials – For infants and toddlers these should be open-ended and freely available as for their older peers: items that support their natural curiosity, items that make sounds or smell, things to be touched, explored and experienced. At this age and stage of development infants and toddlers are motivated by their senses so any materials which support this mode of learning is ideal:

Jo had made some playdough for the infants to explore. She put it on some plastic on the floor and the infants were able to explore it using their hands. Alisha, aged 10 months, picked up a lump and immediately put it to her nose and mouth. She licked it and began to bite the soft dough. She quickly found out that it didn't taste good which Jo acknowledged but continued to put it to her nose and mouth.

Equipment should be clean and age-appropriate; use of treasure baskets and heuristic play is more evident for this age of child. Toys and equipment can be stored in a variety of containers, as with the older children, as these can often become something to explore and play with too. We can all, I'm sure, remember an example of how a young child can spend a great deal of time exploring a box and ignoring the contents!

A range of bricks made from a variety of materials such as soft sponge, wood and plastic all offer different experiences to the children. For the infant they provide a plaything to explore: they grasp, put them to their mouths and bang them together. For the toddler they become items to carry around, stack and knock down again.

Infants and toddlers enjoy movement in their playthings; this could include a range of balls made from a variety of materials including wood, plastic, rubber and fluffy material. Toys with wheels are also popular; children enjoy the motion of them and for the older toddler the fact that they can set them in motion.

Infants and toddlers enjoy a variety of textures. This could include materials which can be bought or sourced from many places and include pieces of material, scarves, socks and flannels, from soft satin and silks to cord and denim. Use of the outdoor space can also offer exploration of textures: the grass, concrete and brick walls all provide fascinating areas to be touched, smelt and tasted.

Infants and toddlers need cosy spaces equipped with soft furnishings; somewhere to snuggle, read a book or just watch their peers with a trusted adult. If space allows a High/Scope setting would endeavour to include a small sofa or large comfy chair; this not only provides a safe, warm space but also reflects home which can offer our youngest children reassurance and comfort. Reminders of home can be particularly comforting for the new or upset child. Items that reflect their home life may include photos of family members or pets and individual comfort items such as dummies and soft blankets.

Soft toys have a place for the young child too. Simple, soft and washable dolls and animals become comforters for the infant and playmates for the toddlers. Equally books, both cloth and board books, support the toddler's early language development and image recognition. All children enjoy the closeness with a familiar adult when sharing a favourite story.

Areas and storage – For our youngest children it is equally important to have basic areas where they can play and explore. These are more likely to use fewer physical partitions to allow the infants and toddlers space to explore their environment. They need open spaces that meet their needs; lets look at a few.

A space to eat and share food is important for all children but infants and toddlers have particular needs. Infants who are bottle-fed need to be fed in a comfortable unhurried way and the practitioner needs to be able to sit comfortably. The quiet comfy area of the room is ideal for this. Toddlers need appropriate-sized tables and chairs to be able to eat together and share the social experience of eating as well as the physical food.

A space to sleep. In some High/Scope settings this can be a separate room especially for this purpose but for most it's a sectioned-off area of the main room. Both should be calm, cosy and relaxing spaces where infants and toddlers can feel safe and secure so they can sleep naturally. Storage for the children's personal belongings needs to be easily accessible to the practitioners settling children for their sleeps. A shelf with labelled baskets or boxes is ideal.

Often next to the sleeping area is the nappy changing area, a space that's not only functional but also can be equipped with pictures and mobiles to keep the infants and toddlers stimulated and interested. Storage for the individual nappies and supplies again should be easily accessible to the practitioner and labelled. The use of children's photos as labels is often used in a High/Scope setting as this allows the toddler to recognise his own things and help get them when a change is needed.

Schedules and routines

Providing a predictable daily schedule and unhurried caregiving routines in an infant-toddler care setting assures children of many opportunities to try out their actions and ideas.

(Post and Hohmann 2000: 192)

As in any early years setting the daily routine in a High/Scope setting is consistent and flexible at the same time: consistent to offer children security in what comes next and to support their organisation and planning of what they wish to do, but also flexible enough to incorporate unplanned-for events such as being able to go outside when it begins to snow, to be able to use all their senses to experience it.

When working with infants and toddlers it's important to follow their natural routines around feeding and sleeping. Practitioners will build a partnership with the parents/carers to ensure the infant's home daily routine is followed as closely as possible but also incorporates the setting ethos and activities. To enable this to happen as smoothly as possible care for infants and toddlers is done in smaller groups; this allows the infants and toddlers to feel secure and safe.

Within the infants and toddlers room the daily routine would have a basic structure but would be equally flexible to accommodate individual needs. This can mean that while some babies may be sleeping others could be enjoying a small- or large-group time or even choice time as indicated on the High/Scope wheel of learning for infants and toddlers.

A sample daily routine for an infant/toddler room may look like this:

Arrival – infants and toddlers arrive at times to suit their family's routines

Breakfast – very important for those who arrive early and would incorporate nappy changing as appropriate

Greeting/large-group time – a chance to say hello and share a song or picture book

Choice time – interesting equipment is available for the infants to explore

Small-group time – practitioners and infants gather to enjoy an activity together in a small group

Outside time – infants and toddlers have opportunity to explore beyond their indoor environment

Lunch – a time to sit together socially, share food and chatter and would incorporate nappy changing as appropriate

Nap time – infants, especially those who stay for the whole day, are supported to rest and sleep if they wish.

A routine of activities as above would be planned for the afternoon. Let's look at each section in more detail:

Arrival

Children arrive at times to suit the family routine; therefore staff need to be available to greet them in a warm and friendly manner. The youngest children (and often the parents) need support through this initial separation and High/Scope practitioners find it helps to acknowledge feelings that both child and parent may be experiencing, for example, 'It's sad when Mummy has to go, isn't it, Thomas?' or 'It's hard when you have to get to work but don't feel ready to leave, Mrs James.' These simple statements can make the difference for both child and parent. There should always be somewhere big enough to hold the children's outdoor clothes, space where they can leave personal belongings – a drawer or box with their name and their photograph or a picture on it, for example. This supports young children's self-esteem and independence; it also welcomes them into the setting and gives them a sense of 'I belong here'. There should be space for parents/carers to pass on information or anecdotes about the child to the setting staff.

Breakfast

A small nutritious breakfast is often offered to the children shortly after they arrive. This offers an opportunity to share food and have a chat.

Greeting/large-group time

With the youngest children large-group time has the same High/Scope ethos in that it's a time to say hello, maybe through a song, share musical experiences and simple stories and dance. Babies particularly enjoy simple books made by the practitioner using photographs of themselves and the setting.

Choice time

This is the main part of the session. It's the chance for infants and toddlers to investigate and explore materials, interact with peers and practitioners and the play environment. It offers them the chance to follow their interests and experience new learning by being active and involved. Practitioners may feel this is similar to the older children's 'work time' in the plan-do-review sequence and in a way it is as the activities are chosen by the infants and toddler and explored and played with in their own way. However, with infants and toddlers there is no formal plan and review times; with older toddlers practitioners may ask, as part of a conversation, 'What are you going to do today?' and chat (maybe over lunch/snack), 'Tell me what you've been doing.' In this way they are preparing the children for the routines in a High/Scope preschool setting but also supporting their thinking and language skills.

During choice time practitioners interact with the infants and toddlers, following their lead and supporting their communication and interaction with peers.

Small-group time

During this time practitioners and infants enjoy an activity together in a small group. The activities are planned around the children's age and stage of development. For the infants and toddlers small-group time can be a great time to use treasure baskets full of interesting items to explore and investigate. These can be made up of items covering themes such as wood, metal or plastic or focused on a colour or texture. Babies particularly enjoy contrast and black and white baskets can prove very popular. In this way the youngest children are introduced to the elements of active learning in an instinctive way using their natural need to explore. Practitioners may also introduce fun messy times using gloop, paint, clay or dough.

Small-group time gives practitioners the opportunity to observe children in the group and listen to their interest; this they can use to write anecdotes to add to the children's development records or to organise the next small-group time.

Outside time

At outside time infants and toddlers have the opportunity to explore beyond their indoor environment. They can experience different textures and use larger pieces of equipment such as playhouses, slides and small climbing structures. Practitioners can make the outdoor space interesting for non-mobile infants by adding wind chimes and mobiles, and for older toddlers the addition of a bird table or an area for digging can be fun. Outside there is also the opportunity to use their large muscle groups through running and using small-wheeled ride-ons or bikes.

Lunch time

This is a time to sit together socially, to share food and chatter. Practitioners support the young children through meal times; for the infants that may be bottle-feeding and for the toddler that may be support with finger foods. Lunchtime should be unhurried and give ample opportunity for the infants and toddlers to eat but also join in with conversations.

Nap/ bodily care times

Throughout the whole of this routine the infants and toddlers' need to sleep or receive a nappy change is incorporated. Practitioners in a High/ Scope setting see nappy changing as another active learning experience for the children. They can use this task as a chance to interact more closely with the infant and use song and rhymes to make it fun. With the older toddler they can be supported to begin to do things for themselves, for example, pull down their trousers in readiness for a change or washing their hands afterwards.

Sleep times are individual to each child; practitioners offer comfort and quiet times for children to rest as they require and most settings have a sleep area with cots for this purpose. This is also an area where the practitioner will link closely with the parent/carer to ensure the infant/ toddler is settled in the way he or she is used to, with his/her comforter and for a length of time that suits both the child and parental wishes.

> Infant and toddler caregivers strive for an overall daily routine that is predictable – organised and consistent – and still flexible enough to accommodate the needs of individual children.
>
> (Post and Hohmann 2000: 195)

Child observation

> At the same time that parents and practitioners are learning about children and each other, each child benefits from the relationships that are developing between adults.
>
> (Post and Hohmann 2000: 295)

In any setting a strong team is essential to ensure a safe, secure active learning environment for young children. This is even more so for infants and toddlers. In a High/Scope setting the ideal is for staff who care for the youngest children to work together as a team to ensure the children are always surrounded by familiar adults even if their key worker is not around. They will spend time planning group times and experiences for the infants and toddlers together, based on observations of the children and their stage of development, being mindful to plan activities that will gently move them on in their progress.

High/Scope advocates that teams spend 30 minutes on a daily basis planning group-time activities for infants and toddlers. This enables them to incorporate recent events and reflect the individual children's interests and stages of development. This can be achieved at quiet times, when children are napping or numbers in the room are lower, and the children can be cared for by cover staff. This may not be practicable for all settings; however, planning as a team should be given some priority.

In the long run, team members are more effective caregivers when they take time together each day to think about what they are observing in children, how they support them and how to solve problems as they arise.

(Post and Hohmann 2000: 304)

When working with the very youngest children the relationship that practitioners build with the parents and carers is vital. The non-verbal infant relies on the caring adults to share information openly about him to ensure his needs are met and that he receives the best possible care and education. Practitioners share development records on a term basis; however, some settings may also use a daily communication book to record for example what the infant has been doing, what they ate, toileting habits. These books allow practitioners to record the day's events so the parent feels included in their child's day and also the family members can record weekend events to share with the setting.

The team of practitioners provide the continuity of care that gives young children the stability and courage to explore, form relationships and develop at their own pace into active learners who are starting out on their learning journey. They support the children's development through planned, stimulating and creative activities and build warm, open relationships with infants and toddlers. As adults who work closely together implementing High/Scope within their setting they are active learners building their knowledge and understanding of very young children.

There are obvious similarities within the High/Scope approach for infants and toddlers and older children. These similarities such as names of areas, segments of the daily routine and continuity of practitioners all support the children we work with to develop confidence, knowledge and creativity as they begin their journeys into formal learning.

How High/Scope links to the Early Years Foundation Stage

The High/Scope approach, as outlined in the previous chapters, provides young children with a developmentally appropriate curriculum with active learning at its core. For all children High/Scope believes that 'children gain confidence, initiative and love of lifelong learning when involved in well supported activities of their own choosing' (Bell 2004: 5).

Over the years successive governments have made changes to the way our youngest children have been taught and supported on their learning journey. This has resulted in curriculum guidance documents that lay out and inform the way practitioners work with children:

- In 1999 the early learning goals were published. These goals identified the expectations for children in six areas of learning prior to Year 1 of formal education.

- In September 2000 the introduction of the Foundation Stage for children from 3 years to the end of reception class in mainstream schooling introduced practitioners to the stepping stones, which supported children on their journey into education. These stepping stones identified the progress for children towards the early learning goals in terms of knowledge, understanding, skills and attitudes.

- In 2007 the introduction of the Early Years Foundation Stage pulled together two previous documents – the *Birth to Three Matters* and the

Foundation Stage Profile – thereby setting out a framework for children, from birth to the end of their reception year education, which supports and guides practitioners in their work.

As a philosophy and well-researched curriculum the High/Scope approach encompasses the early learning goals for young children in an effective and supportive way. Through active learning and the key developmental indicators children's ongoing opportunities for learning and development are fostered in a natural systematic way. High/Scope practitioners will use the early learning goals within the EYFS alongside the key developmental indicators and observations and interests of the children, to inform their planning of activities for the children in their care.

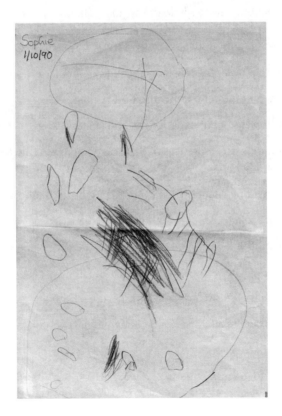

Let's look in turn at each early learning goal, which are core to the Early Years Foundation Stage for children, and see how they link with the High/Scope approach. By linking the individual key developmental indicators to when or how children's development through active learning occurs, you can see the way the High/Scope curriculum fully supports the early learning goals.

Personal, social and emotional development

This area of development is crucial for all young children as it can have an effect on all other areas of learning. All practitioners strive to enable children to develop a positive sense of themselves. Through the Early Years Foundation Stage early learning goals children are expected to:

- be interested and motivated to learn
- be confident, initiate ideas and speak in a familiar group
- maintain attention and concentration
- respond to significant experiences and show a range of feelings
- be developing an awareness of their own needs and the feelings and wishes of others
- developing a respect for their culture and those of others
- be forming relationships with adults and peers
- work as part of a group, take turns and share
- have an understanding of right and wrong and why
- consider how their words and actions affect others
- dress and undress themselves, manage their own personal hygiene
- select and use resources
- understand others' needs, views and cultures and treat them respectfully

- expect that others will treat their views, needs and culture with respect.

These traits are supported by the High/Scope foundation key developmental indicators of *approaches to learning; social and emotional development; language, literacy and communication;* and *social studies.* High/Scope believes that 'children's ability to follow through on their intentions is closely related to their developing ability to relate to others (High/Scope UK 2001: 31).

Within the High/Scope key developmental indicator **approaches to learning** children have opportunity to:

- make and express their choices, plans and decisions through the plan-do-review process

- solve problems encountered in play by use of the six steps to conflict resolution.

Within the High/Scope key developmental indicator **social and emotional development** children have opportunity to:

- take care of their own needs by being supported by adults who share control with children

- build relationships with children and adults through shared control

- create and experience collaborative play in their work (do) time

- deal with social conflict using the six steps to conflict resolution

- express feelings in words at review time and through the approach to conflict.

Within the High/Scope key developmental indicator **language, literacy and communication** children have the opportunity to:

- talk with others about personally meaningful experiences at review time and in large-group times

- describe objects, events and relations throughout the High/Scope session.

And within the High/Scope key developmental indicator **social studies** children have the opportunity to:

- be sensitive to the feelings, interests, viewpoints and needs of others through consistent exposure to a problem-solving approach to conflict and from the example of the practitioners around them

- participate in group routines through small- and large-group times.

Communication, language and literacy

Communicating with others is fundamental in human development. Children communicate first through sounds and actions which soon develop into recognisable speech and understanding of the written word. Through the EYFS early learning goals children are expected to:

- interact with others, negotiate plans and activities and take turns in conversations

- enjoy listening to and using spoken and written language

- be able to respond to what they have heard with comments, questions or actions

- listen to and enjoy stories, songs, poems, rhymes and make up their own

- extend their vocabulary

- speak clearly with confidence, showing an awareness of the listener

- use language to imagine, recreate roles and experiences

- use talk to organise, sequence and clarify their thinking ideas, feelings and events

- hear and say letter sounds in order, linking the sounds to the letters and naming them

- use phonic knowledge to write simple words and attempt more complex words

- explore words, sounds and text

- retell narratives in the correct order

- retell familiar words and simple sentences

- know that print has meaning and English is read from left to right and top to bottom

- show an understanding of stories and be able to answer questions such as who, where, why and how in regard to the story

- attempt writing for purpose, such as lists, stories and instructions

- write their own name and other common labels and begin to form simple sentences

- use and hold a pencil to write recognisable letters.

These traits are supported by the High/Scope key developmental indicators of *approaches to learning; social and emotional development; language, literacy and communication*; and *social studies* and *the arts – dramatic and music*. High/Scope believes that children's developing language is a lively process of discovery that involves all those in contact with young children; it can be fostered through the active learning approach.

Within the High/Scope key developmental indicator **approaches to learning** children have the opportunity to:

- make and express their choices, plans and decisions through the plan-do-review process.

Within the High/Scope key developmental indicator **social and emotional development** children have the opportunity to:

- express feelings in words at review time, group times and through the approach to conflict

- participate in group routines through small and large group times

- build relationships with children and adults through shared control

- create and experience collaborative play in their work (do) time.

Within the High/Scope key developmental indicator **language, literacy and communication** children have the opportunity to:

- talk with others about meaningful experiences in review time and large-group times

- describe objects, events and relations in review time and large-group time

- have fun with language: listening to stories and poems, making up stories and rhymes, retelling stories; all can be done in large-group times and at review times

- dictate stories at story time in large- or small-group time

- write in various ways: drawing, scribbling, letter-like forms, invented spelling, conventional forms; can happen in the art area, on the computer or when children begin to write their own plans

- read in various ways: reading books, signs, symbols and one's own handwriting; this happens during work time in the book area or on the computer and throughout the setting where equipment is labelled.

Within the High/Scope key developmental indicator **social studies** children have the opportunity to:

- participate in group routines through small- and large-group times.

Within the High/Scope key developmental indicator **the arts – dramatic art** children have the opportunity to:

- pretend and role play with supportive adult throughout work time and in small-group time experiences

- imitate actions and sounds within group times and work (do) time.

And within the High/Scope key developmental indicator *the arts – music* children have the opportunity to:

- explore and identify sounds through interaction with simple instruments and equipment such as radios and CD players

- explore their singing voice at group times.

Preschool children are powerfully motivated to communicate with others through conversation. They also enjoy such highly literate pursuits as writing and reading in their own particular ways.

(Hohmann and Weikart 2002: 342)

Problem solving, reasoning and numeracy

Young children develop their mathematical thinking through continuing opportunities with real materials that interest and inspire them. Through exploration, experimentation and talk with others children develop their ability to count, sort, match, recognise pattern, shape, number and measure.

Through the stepping stones to the Foundation Stage early learning goals children are expected to:

- say and use number names in order

- count reliably up to 10

- recognise numerals 1 to 9

- use developing maths to solve practical problems

- begin to use adding and subtracting vocabulary

- use 'more' and 'less' when comparing numbers

- find one more or one less than a number from 1 to 10

- begin to link addition to joining two groups of things and subtraction to taking away

- use quantifying language e.g. greater, smaller, heavier, lighter

- talk about, create and recognise simple patterns

- use shape and size language e.g. circle, square, bigger, smaller

- use everyday words to describe position.

These traits are supported by the High/Scope key developmental indicators of *arts and science* incorporating *mathematics – number, seriation and space* and *science and technology – classification*. Children need a continuing and varied range of materials and experiences to develop their mathematical thinking and understanding. Within the High/Scope curriculum children are supported to experiment, explore and discuss their findings with interested adults.

Within the High/Scope key developmental indicator **arts and science – number** children have the opportunity to:

● compare the number of things in two sets to determine 'more', 'fewer', 'same amount' by exposure to a range of equipment that can be sorted e.g. farm/wild animals, small bricks and natural materials like fir cones and stones

● arrange two sets of objects in one-to-one correspondence as in the home area matching up cups and saucers and pans with their lids

● count objects throughout the daily routine as and when it occurs.

Within the High/Scope key developmental indicator **arts and science – seriation** children have the opportunity to:

● compare attributes (longer, shorter, bigger, smaller) through manipulation of materials such as clay and playdough, through building towers and looking at themselves in relation to their peers

● arrange several things one after another in a series or pattern and describe the relationship (big/bigger/biggest, red/blue/red/blue) through natural play in the home area and threading with beads

● fit one ordered set of objects to another through trial and error e.g. matching up cups and saucers within the home area, small with small, big with big.

Within the High/Scope key developmental indicator **arts and science – space** children have the opportunity to:

● fill and empty within work time at the sand and water tray and when pouring their own drinks at snack/lunch time

● fit things together and take them apart; through use of puzzles, a variety of bricks and magnetic connections on train sets

● observe people, things and places from different special viewpoints; this can happen during physical time when children move from the floor to climbing on frames or up trees or when looking at pictures in books and photographs

● experience and describe positions, directions and distances in the play space, building and neighbourhood; when walking to and from the setting, when out on walks around the setting and in the outdoor play space

● interpret spatial relations in drawings, pictures and photographs during large-group time and when sharing a cosy story with practitioners.

And within the High/Scope key developmental indicator **science and technology – classification** children have the opportunity to:

● explore and describe similarities, differences and the attributes of things through the range of activities and equipment available to children at all times and in interactions with practitioners and peers

● distinguish and describe shapes both within the play space and through outside experiences

● sort and match through play with a range of toys and equipment e.g. home area cutlery and crockery, beads and bricks and tidying the play space after use

● use and describe something in several ways through the use of natural materials e.g. fir cones, that can one day be things to cook and the next things to line up a fence for your farm

● hold more than one attribute in mind by interacting with equipment such as bricks where you have both shape and colour to define them

● distinguish between 'some' and 'all' through games and group times.

Knowledge and understanding of the world

This area of learning supports children to develop knowledge, skills and understanding to make sense of the world around them. It gives them insight into later concepts such as science, design and technology, history, geography, information and communication technology.

Through the EYFS early learning goals children are expected to:

- investigate objects and materials using their senses

- find out about and identify some features of living things, objects and events

- look closely at patterns, similarities and differences

- ask 'why' questions

- build and construct using appropriate materials and adapt where necessary

- select and use appropriate tools

- find out and use information and communication technology to support their learning

- find out about past events in their own lives and of those around them

- observe and discover about the community they live in and the wider world

- find out about their environment and their likes and dislikes

- begin to have knowledge of their own culture and beliefs and those of others.

These traits are supported by the High/Scope key developmental indicators of *approaches to learning; language, literacy and communication; social and emotional development; mathematics – seriation, space; science and technology – classification, time; social studies*; and *the arts – visual and dramatic.*

Children's knowledge of the world, their personal culture and the society they live in will be constructed through creative, ongoing interactions with people, materials and ideas. They will act upon their innate desire to explore, ask and search for answers to questions and solve problems that stand in their way in order to further their understanding and be a key player in their own learning.

(High/Scope UK 2001: 54)

Within the High/Scope key developmental indicator **approaches to learning** children have the opportunity to:

● make and express their choices, plans and decisions through the plan-do-review process

● solve problems encountered in play through discussion with those around them, both children and adults, and the use of the six steps to conflict resolution.

Within the High/Scope key developmental indicator **language, literacy and communication** children have the opportunity to:

● talk with others about personally meaningful experiences both at large-group times and on a one-to-one basis with practitioners throughout the session

● describe objects, events and relations; at review time children are supported to talk about what they have been doing.

Within the High/Scope key developmental indicator **social and emotional development** children have the opportunity to:

● express feelings in words at review time and through the approach to conflict resolution

● build relationships with children and adults through shared control and treating each other with kindness and respect.

Within the High/Scope key developmental indicator *arts and science – seriation* children have the opportunity to:

- compare attributes (longer, shorter, bigger, smaller) through manipulation of materials such as clay and playdough, through building towers and looking at themselves in relation to their peers.

Within the High/Scope key developmental indicator *arts and science – space* children have the opportunity to:

- fill and empty within work time at the sand and water tray and when pouring their own drinks at snack/lunch time

- fit things together and take them apart; through use of puzzles, a variety of bricks and magnetic connections on train sets

- change the shape and arrangement of objects (wrapping, twisting, stretching, stacking, enclosing) by use of materials such as tape, paper, wool/thread, cloth and rope; children can also experience this through play with clay and dough

- observe people, places and things from different spatial viewpoints; this can happen during physical time when children move from the floor to climbing on frames or up trees or when looking at pictures in books and photographs.

Within the High/Scope key developmental indicator *science and technology – classification* children have the opportunity to:

- recognise objects by sight, sound, touch and smell through games played at group times (e.g. Kim's game and sound lotto), by use of photographs and cookery/snack time experiences

- explore and describe similarities, differences and the attributes of things through the range of activities and equipment available to children at all times and in interactions with practitioners and peers

- sort and match through play with a range of toys and equipment e.g. home area cutlery and crockery, beads and bricks and tidying the play space after use

- use and describe something in several ways through the use of natural materials e.g. fir cones, that can one day be things to cook and the next things to line up a fence for your farm

- describe characteristics something does not possess or what class it does not belong to through matching games and use of a wide range of play equipment such as bricks, wild and farm animals and shapes.

Within the High/Scope key developmental indicator **science and technology – time** children have the opportunity to:

- experience and compare time intervals through exposure to a consistent daily routine, when looking forward to events such as birthdays and holidays, backwards when recalling events and use of timers/time signals

- anticipate, remember and describe sequences of events through pictorial and written record of setting events such as trips or visitors, the visual daily routine displayed in the setting and review time.

Within the High/Scope key developmental indicator **social studies** children have the opportunity to:

- be sensitive to the feelings, interests, viewpoints and needs of others through consistent exposure to a problem-solving approach to conflict and from the example of the practitioners around them.

Within the High/Scope key developmental indicator **the arts – visual art** children have the opportunity to:

- relate models, pictures and photographs to real places and things when going on walks in the community

- make models out of clay, blocks and other materials at work time through choice or at small-group times.

And finally, within the High/Scope key developmental indicator *the arts – dramatic art* children have the opportunity to:

● pretend and role play through the availability of equipment throughout the setting.

Physical development

Children are innately physical from before they are born; therefore this mode of learning is essential and natural in the early years. Babies and young children need to develop their physical skills of coordination and movement through experience. Through their developing senses they learn about and from 'their' world and make connections between new and existing knowledge. Physical development also supports the positive benefits of being active and healthy both in body and mind.

Through the EYFS early learning goals children are expected to:

● move with confidence, imagination and in safety

● move with control and coordination

● travel around, under, over and through balancing and climbing equipment

● show an awareness of space, themselves and others

● recognise the importance of being healthy

● recognise the changes that happen to their bodies when they are active

● use a range of equipment

● use tools, construction and malleable materials with control and safely.

These traits are supported by the High/Scope key developmental indicators of *physical development, health and well-being; the arts – visual, dramatic and music; mathematics – space; science and technology – time and classification; social and emotional development; language, literacy and communication; approaches to learning;* and *social studies.* A High/

Scope active learning environment supports their desire to move and gives them opportunities to develop coordination, control and confidence in their individual abilities.

Within the High/Scope key developmental indicator *physical development, health and well-being* children have the opportunity to:

● move in non-locomotor ways (anchored movement: bending, twisting, rocking, swinging your arms) through movement games both indoor and outside; adults acknowledge for children their movements within play

● move in locomotor ways (non-anchored movement: running, jumping, hopping, skipping, marching, climbing) through outside opportunities in the play space and use of a large block area indoors

● move with objects through the use of scarves, hoops, balloons and streamers; through introducing objects to push and pull such as wheelbarrows and pushchairs and availability of a variety of balls

● express creativity in movement through review time and in ideas about how to move from one activity to another in transition times

● act upon movement direction within physical education and movement times and during group times or games

● feel and express a steady beat at singing times and use of music tapes/ CDs/recording equipment; children can also experience this when using a rocking horse or even just walking to and around the setting

● move in sequences to a common beat through simple two-step actions at singing or movement time such as jumping with legs open then closed and using the words 'open', 'shut' as you jump.

Within the High/Scope key developmental indicator *the arts – music* children have the opportunity to:

● move to music at singing times, movement times and through access to radio/tape recorders

● to play simple musical instruments in a group, with peers and alone.

Within the High/Scope key developmental indicator **the arts – visual art** children have the opportunity to:

- make models out of clay, blocks and other materials at work time through choice or at small group times

- draw and paint with a wide range of equipment in the art area but also on the computer; children's work is valued and displayed around the setting.

Within the High/Scope key developmental indicator **the arts – dramatic art** children have the opportunity to:

- imitate actions and sounds at review time, using action rhymes and stories and through observation of the people and animals in the world around them.

Within the High/Scope key developmental indicator **arts and science – space** children have the opportunity to:

- observe people, things and places from different special viewpoints; this can happen during physical time when children move from the floor to climbing on frames or up trees or when looking at pictures in books and photographs

- experience and describe positions, directions and distances in the play space, building and neighbourhood; when walking to and from the setting, when out on walks around the setting and in the outdoor play space

- change the shape and arrangement of objects (wrapping, twisting, stretching, stacking, enclosing) by use of materials such as tape, paper, wool/thread, cloth and rope; children can also experience this through play with clay and dough.

Within the High/Scope key developmental indicator **– science and technology – time** children have the opportunity to:

- anticipate, remember and describe sequences of events through pictorial and written record of setting events such as trips or visitors, the visual daily routine displayed in the setting and review time

- experience and describe rates of movement through use of materials that they can set in motion such as water/sand wheels and friction cars

- start and stop an action on signal through use of time warnings throughout the daily routine and equipment such as alarm clocks and sand timers

- experience and compare time intervals through exposure of a consistent daily routine, when looking forward to events such as birthdays and holidays and use of timers/time signals.

Within the High/Scope key developmental indicator *social and emotional development* children have the opportunity to:

- take care of their own needs by being supported by adults who share control with children

- create and experience collaborative play in their work (do) time by providing space that encourages children to play together e.g. in the house and block area

- express feelings in words at review time and through the approach to conflict.

Within the High/Scope key developmental indicator *language, literacy and communication* children have the opportunity to:

- talk with others about personally meaningful experiences both at large-group times and on a one-to-one basis with practitioners throughout the session

- write in various ways: drawing, scribbling, letter-like forms, invented spelling, conventional forms; can happen in the art area, on the computer or when children begin to write their own plans.

Within the High/Scope key developmental indicator *approaches to learning* children have the opportunity to:

- solve problems encountered in play through discussion with those around them, both children and adults, and the use of the six steps to conflict resolution.

And within the High/Scope key developmental indicator *social studies* children have the opportunity to:

- be sensitive to the feelings, interests, viewpoints and needs of others again with continued exposure to a problem-solving approach to conflict and from the example of the practitioners around them.

Creative development

Creativity plays an important role in children's play and development. Through being creative children build connections between other areas of learning therefore supporting their developing understanding and knowledge.

Through the EYFS early learning goals children are expected to:

- explore colour, shape, texture, form and space in both two and three dimensions

- recognise and explore how sounds can be changed, recognise repeated sounds and sound patterns and match movements to music

- use their imagination through art, design, music, dance role play and stories

- respond in a variety of ways to what they feel, see, touch, smell and hear

- express and communicate their ideas, thoughts and feelings using a wide range of tools, materials and experiences.

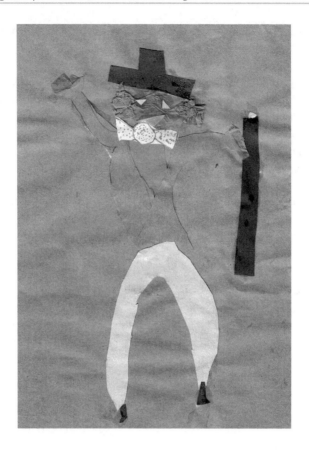

These traits are supported by the High/Scope key developmental indicators of *science and technology – classification; the arts – visual art, dramatic art, music; physical development, health and well-being; arts and science – space; language, literacy and communication; social and emotional development; approaches to learning;* and *social studies.*

Creative Representation – the process of constructing mental images of actual objects, people and experiences – enables young children to express an understanding of their world through pretend play, model making, drawing and painting.

(Hohmann and Weikart 2002: 310)

Within the High/Scope key developmental indicator **science and technology – classification** children have the opportunity to:

- recognise objects by sight, sound, touch and smell through games played at group times (e.g. Kim's game and sound lotto), by use of photographs and cookery/snack time experiences.

Within the High/Scope key developmental indicator **the arts – visual art** children have the opportunity to:

- relate models, pictures and photographs to real places and things when going on walks in the community

- make models out of clay, blocks and other materials at work time through choice or at small-group times

- draw and paint with a wide range of equipment in the art area but also on the computer; children's work is valued and displayed around the setting.

Within the High/Scope key developmental indicator **the arts – dramatic art** children have the opportunity to:

- pretend and role play through the availability of equipment throughout the setting and the interaction with supportive adults who join in the children's world

- imitate actions and sounds at review time, using action rhymes and stories and through observation of the people and animals in the world around them.

Within the High/Scope key developmental indicator **the arts – music** children have the opportunity to:

- move to music at singing times, movement times and through access to radio/CD players/tape recorders

- explore and identify sounds through sound guessing games, by playing musical instruments and listening to natural sounds from the environment

● explore one's own singing voice at regular times with songs and rhymes; practitioners support children to make sounds; use of a tape recorder can be fun

● develop melody through playing 'guess the tune' type games when both adults and children take turns in humming or singing and guessing

● sing songs at regular large-group times and access to music tapes or CDs in the setting; practitioners using songs to signal a move from one activity to another and supporting children to write their own songs

● play simple musical instruments by having a music area (if space allows) or regular music times, large-group and small-group times and at transition times.

Within the High/Scope key developmental indicator **physical development, health and well-being** children have the opportunity to:

● move in non-locomotor ways (anchored movement: bending, twisting, rocking, swinging your arms) through movement games both indoor and outside; adults acknowledge for children their movements within play

● move in locomotor ways (non-anchored movement: running, jumping, hopping, skipping, marching, climbing) through outside opportunities in the play space and use of a large block area indoors

● express creativity in movement through review time and in ideas about how to move from one activity to another/transition times

● act upon movement direction within physical education/movement times and during group times and games

● feel and express a steady beat at singing times and use of music tapes/ CDs/recorder; children can also experience this when using a rocking horse or even just walking to and around the setting

- describe movement at large-group times by joining in with action rhymes, at plan-do-review times when talking about what they have been doing and through sensitive adult questions

- move in sequences to a common beat through simple two-step actions at singing or movement times such as jumping with legs open then closed and using the words 'open', 'shut' as you jump

- move with objects through the use of scarves, hoops, balloons and streamers; through introducing objects to push and pull such as wheelbarrows and pushchairs and availability of a variety of balls.

Within the High/Scope key developmental indicator *arts and science – space* children have the opportunity to:

- change the shape and arrangement of objects (wrapping, twisting, stretching, stacking, enclosing) by use of materials such as tape, paper, wool/thread, cloth and rope; children can also experience this through play with clay and dough

- experience and describe positions, directions and distances in the play space, building and neighbourhood; when walking to and from the setting, when out on walks around the setting and in the outdoor play space

- interpret spatial relations in drawings, pictures and photographs during large-group time and when sharing a cosy story with practitioners through the use and availability of materials at review time; photographs of children in action are particularly useful.

Within the High/Scope key developmental indicator *language, literacy and communication* children have the opportunity to:

- talk with others about personally meaningful experiences both at large-group times and on a one-to-one basis with practitioners throughout the session

- have fun with language: listening to stories and poems, making up stories and rhymes, retelling stories; all can be done in large-group times and at review times

- describe objects, events and relations; at review time children are supported to talk about what they have been doing.

Within the High/Scope key developmental indicator **social and emotional development** children have the opportunity to:

- create and experience collaborative play in their work (do) time by providing space that encourages children to play together e.g. in the house and block area

- express feelings in words at review time and through the approach to conflict resolution.

Within the High/Scope key developmental indicator **approaches to learning** children have the opportunity to:

- make and express their choices, plans and decisions through the plan-do-review process.

And within the High/Scope key developmental indicator **social studies** children have the opportunity to:

- be sensitive to the feelings, interests, viewpoints and needs of others through consistent exposure to a problem-solving approach to conflict and from the example of the practitioners around them.

As this chapter shows, the High/Scope approach fully supports the Early Years Foundation Stage early learning goals. Children in an active learning setting are supported and encouraged to experience a diverse range of experiences that support their individual and unique level of understanding and stage of development. Practitioners observe children throughout their play and work, offering appropriate support and joining with the children as requested. They use both the stepping stones to the early learning goals and the High/Scope key developmental indicators to guide them in their work with young children.

Intrinsic motivation is central to children having positive attitudes and dispositions to learning. Children who systematically have experience of the High/Scope Approach see themselves as capable learners whose work and effort will often lead to success.

(High/Scope UK 2001: 8)

Finda   and   Sophie.

Appendix

The High/Scope "Wheel" plus High/Scope UK "Tyre"

FAMILY INCLUSION

* Recognition of key role of the family
* Unique culture of the child and family
* Family Strengths

ASSESSMENT

ADULT-CHILD INTERACTION

* Authentic relationships

* Access to the Curriculum

* Teamwork
* Daily Anecdotal Notes
* Daily Planning
* Child Assessment
* Partnership with parents

* Interaction Strategies
* Encouragement
* Problem-Solving Approach to Conflict

* Responsive Adult

ACTIVE LEARNING

Initiative

Key Experiences

DAILY ROUTINES

LEARNING ENVIRONMENT

* Criteria for Quality

* Plan-Do-Review
* Small-Group Time
* Large-Group Time
* Greeting Time

* Areas
* Materials
* Storage

* Ongoing support and training

* Developmentally Valid Curriculum

* Early Learning Goals & Life Long Learning Benefits

RESEARCH

The High/Scope Wheel & Tyre (UK) for Children with Special Needs / Additional Needs

FAMILY INCLUSION
* Recognition of key role of the family
* Unique culture of the child and family
* Family Strengths

ASSESSMENT | ADULT-CHILD INTERACTION

* Access to the Approach

* Teamwork
  –Key Worker System
* Daily Anecdotal Notes
  –Supports recording of progress on individual Education Plan
* Daily Planning
  –Supports implementation Individual Education Plan
* Child Assessment

* Interaction Strategies
  –Knowledge of speech & language delay and disorder
* Encouragement
  –Differences in motivation
  –Differences in how children with SEN learn
* Problem-Solving Approach to Conflict
  –Model how to solve problems

* Authentic relationships

* Responsive Adult

ACTIVE LEARNING
* Initiative
  –INDEPENDENCE
  –Making choices
* Key Experiences
  –Adapted Key Experiences

DAILY ROUTINES

* Criteria for Quality

* Plan-Do-Review
  –Developmental sequences
* Small-Group-Time
  –Consideration of individual needs within a group
* Large-Group-Time
  –Visual Cues
  –Signing

LEARNING ENVIRONMENT

* Areas
  –Ideally lots of space
  –Clear boundaries
  –Distraction-free
* Materials
  –Developmentally appropriate
  –Sensory materials
  –Motivating
  –Safety concerns
  –Specialist equipment
* Storage
  –Accessibility
  –Labelling: real objects pictures symbols

* Ongoing support and training

* Developmentally Valid Curriculum

* Early Learning Goals & Life Long Learning Benefits

RESEARCH

© Adapted from High/Scope Foundation "Wheel of Learning"
Additions to The High/Scope Wheel: Adaptations for Children with SEN (1998)
Dr. Julia Watson, Medecroft Opportunity Centre, Hampshire Education Authority.
© High/Scope UK, 2002

The High/Scope Infant and Toddler "Wheel of Learning"

Reproduced with kind permission from High/Scope UK
© 2002 High/Scope UK

High/Scope Preschool Curriculum Content

Approaches to Learning
• Making and expressing choices, plans, and decisions
• Solving problems encountered in play

Language, Literacy, and Communication
• Talking with others about personally meaningful experiences
• Describing objects, events, and relations
• Having fun with language: listening to stories and poems, making up stories and rhymes
• Writing in various ways: drawing, scribbling, and using letterlike forms, invented spelling, and conventional forms
• Reading in various ways: reading storybooks, signs and symbols, and one's own writing
• Dictating stories

Social and Emotional Development
• Taking care of one's own needs
• Expressing feelings in words
• Building relationships with children and adults
• Creating and experiencing collaborative play
• Dealing with social conflict

Physical Development, Health, and Well-Being
• Moving in nonlocomotor ways (anchored movement: bending, twisting, rocking, swinging one's arms)
• Moving in locomotor ways (nonanchored movement: running, jumping, hopping, skipping, marching, climbing)
• Moving with objects
• Expressing creativity in movement
• Describing movement
• Acting upon movement directions
• Feeling and expressing steady beat
• Moving in sequences to a common beat

Arts and Sciences

Mathematics

Seriation
• Comparing attributes (longer/shorter, bigger/smaller)
• Arranging several things one after another in a series or pattern and describing the relationships (big/bigger/biggest, red/blue/red/blue)
• Fitting one ordered set of objects to another through trial and error (small cup and small saucer, medium cup and medium saucer, big cup and big saucer)

Number
• Comparing the numbers of things in two sets to determine "more," "fewer," "same number"
• Arranging two sets of objects in one-to-one correspondence
• Counting objects

Space
• Filling and emptying
• Fitting things together and taking them apart
• Changing the shape and arrangement of objects (wrapping, twisting, stretching, stacking, enclosing)
• Observing people, places, and things from different spatial viewpoints
• Experiencing and describing positions, directions, and distances in the play space, building, and neighborhood
• Interpreting spatial relations in drawings, pictures, and photographs

Key developmental indicators (KDIs) are the building blocks of thinking and reasoning at each stage of development. High/Scope identifies 58 preschool KDIs organized under five content areas.

Science and Technology

Classification
• Recognizing objects by sight, sound, touch, taste, and smell
• Exploring and describing similarities, differences, and the attributes of things
• Distinguishing and describing shapes
• Sorting and matching
• Using and describing something in several ways
• Holding more than one attribute in mind at a time
• Distinguishing between "some" and "all"
• Describing characteristics something does not possess or what class it does not belong to

Time
• Starting and stopping an action on signal
• Experiencing and describing rates of movement
• Experiencing and comparing time intervals
• Anticipating, remembering, and describing sequences of events

Social Studies
• Participating in group routines
• Being sensitive to the feelings, interests, and needs of others

The Arts

Visual Art
• Relating models, pictures, and photographs to real places and things
• Making models out of clay, blocks, and other materials
• Drawing and painting

Dramatic Art
• Imitating actions and sounds
• Pretending and role playing

Music
• Moving to music
• Exploring and identifying sounds
• Exploring the singing voice
• Developing melody
• Singing songs
• Playing simple musical instruments

High/Scope Key Experiences For Infants and Toddlers

Sense of Self
- Expressing initiative
- Distinguishing "me" from others
- Solving problems encountered in exploration and play
- Doing things for themselves

Social Relations
- Forming attachment to a primary caregiver
- Building relationships with other adults
- Building relationships with peers
- Expressing emotions
- Showing empathy toward the feelings and needs of others
- Developing social play

Creative Representation
- Imitating and pretending
- Exploring building and art materials
- Responding to and identifying pictures and photographs

Movement
- Moving parts of the body (head-turning, grasping, kicking)
- Moving the whole body (rolling, crawling, cruising, walking, running, balancing)
- Moving with objects
- Feeling and expressing steady beat

Music
- Listening to music
- Responding to music
- Exploring and imitating sounds
- Exploring vocal pitch sounds

Communication and Language
- Listening and responding
- Communicating nonverbally
- Participating in communication give and take
- Communicating verbally
- Exploring picture books and magazines
- Enjoying stories, rhymes, and songs

Exploring Objects
- Exploring objects with the hands, feet, mouth, eyes, ears, and nose
- Discovering object permanence
- Exploring and noticing how things are the same or different

Early Quantity and Number
- Experiencing "more"
- Experiencing one-to-one correspondence
- Experiencing the number of things

Space
- Exploring and noticing location of objects
- Observing people and things from various perspectives
- Filling and emptying, putting in and taking out
- Taking things apart and fitting them together

Time
- Anticipating familiar events
- Noticing the beginning and ending of time intervals
- Experiencing "fast" and "slow"
- Repeating an action to make something happen again, experiencing cause and effect

From *Tender Care and Early Learning* (p. 38) by Jacalyn Post and Mary Hohmann Ypslanti, High/Scope Press 2000. High/Scope Educational Research Foundation. Used with permission.

References, further reading and training opportunities

References

Bell, Jos. (2004) *The High/Scope Approach in Practice – Twenty Years Experience in the UK*. London: High/Scope UK.

Evans, Betsy. (2002) *You Can't Come to My birthday Party!* Ypsilanti, MI: High/Scope Press.

High/Scope UK. (2001) *High/Scope and the Curriculum Guidance for the Foundation Stage – Providing the Process for the Early Learning Goals*. London: High/Scope UK.

Hohmann, Mary and Weikart, David P. (2002) *Educating Young Children*. Ypsilanti, MI: High/Scope Press.

Post, Jacalyn and Hohmann, Mary. (2000) *Tender Care and Early Learning*. Ypsilanti, MI: High/Scope Press.

Schweinhart, Lawrence J, Montie, Jeanne, Xiang, Zongping, Barnett, W. Steven, Belfield, Clive. R and Nores, Milagros. (2005) *Lifetime Effects: The High/Scope Perry Preschool Study Through Age 40*. Ypsilanti, MI: High/Scope Press.

Weikart, David P. (2004) *How High/Scope Grew – A Memoir*. Ypsilanti, MI: High/Scope Press.

Further reading

If this book has inspired you to seek out further information on the High/ Scope approach I would recommend you obtain a copy of *Educating Young Children* by Mary Hohmann and David Weikart. This book comprehensively takes the reader through the approach in a practical and specific way, offering strategies for adults to make active learning a reality in their settings. It includes amongst other things anecdotes, photographs and suggestions that reflect not only research from within the High/Scope Educational Research Foundation but also from settings across the USA and worldwide.

For further information and guidance on High/Scope when working with infants and toddlers I suggest *Tender Care and Early Learning* by Jacalyn Post and Mary Hohmann.

Both books can be obtained from High/Scope UK (details below).

Enquiries regarding training opportunities

For settings and/or practitioners who wish to fully embrace the High/ Scope philosophy, training in the High/Scope approach is necessary. Information about training can be obtained from:

High/Scope UK
High/Scope National Training and Demonstration Centre
South Tyneside Early Excellence Children's Centre
Campbell Park Road
Hebburn
Tyne and Wear
NE31 1QY

TEL: 0870 777 7680/7681
Email: highscope@btconnect.com
www.high-scope.org.uk

High/Scope UK can offer a range of training from introductory days or half-days to the full High/Scope Curriculum Implementation Course. They are also the centre for training experienced practitioners as endorsed trainers to offer more localised training opportunities to settings.